Misunderstood Vegetables

Misunderstood Vegetables

How to Fall in Love with Sunchokes, Rutabaga, Eggplant, and More

Becky Selengut

PHOTOGRAPHY BY CLARE BARBOZA

Countryman Press

An Imprint of W. W. Norton & Company
Celebrating a Century of Independent Publishing

.

For information about permission to reproduce selections from this book, write to
Permissions, Countryman Press, 500 Fifth Avenue, New York, NY 10110

For information about special discounts for bulk purchases, please contact
W. W. Norton Special Sales at specialsales@wwnorton.com or 800-233-4830

Manufacturing by Versa Press
Book design by Allison Chi
Production manager: Devon Zahn

Countryman Press
www.countrymanpress.com

An imprint of W. W. Norton & Company, Inc.
500 Fifth Avenue, New York, NY 10110
www.wwnorton.com

978-1-68268-803-8

10 9 8 7 6 5 4 3 2 1

To my alma mater, the Seattle Culinary Academy, and their publicly funded, low-cost, and accessible programming and, specifically, to the passionate, hardworking teachers who dedicate their lives to educating and mentoring the next generation of culinary professionals.

Contents

What Is a Misunderstood Vegetable?

1. Any vegetable that you keep walking by in the supermarket or at a farmers' market and you have no idea what the bloody hell to do with it, if you even know what it is in the first place.

2. A vegetable that you've cooked or eaten once or twice and you think the texture is weird or it's bitter or you just don't like it, but you may have only had it prepared improperly.

3. A vegetable that you can think of only one or two uses for.

Introduction

"What on earth is that hideous thing?" asked the grocery checker.

Their name tag said CHRIS. HI, I'M NEW! I laughed and picked up the filthy softball-sized bulb, its skinny roots like a dozen ballerina legs twisted into impossible positions. I started to tell them it was celeriac and then quickly edited myself and said, "It's a celery root, a cousin of celery. It's probably this unattractive on the outside because it knows just how good it is on the inside." Chris held it up in the air, just staring at it.

They picked up a smallish white orb with greens on the top. "Turnip?"

"That," I said, "is the most beautiful vegetable in the entire store."

Chris blinked at me because it looked just so-so on the outside. "Seriously, cut it open and you'll be amazed! It's a watermelon radish, and it's incredible looking."

"I don't think I know the code to this, but I trust you," Chris said, smiling, flipping through the price look-up book.

I felt like an enthusiastic ambassador for unusual produce, and not just to Chris. These moments kept happening, prepping for a dinner party with friends, standing next to someone at a farmers' market, overhearing their questions and puzzled looks. And then a light bulb went off.

Starting in 2018, I began teaching a class, Misunderstood Vegetables, at The Pantry, a cooking school in Seattle. I changed the menus seasonally and I slapped googly eyes on the featured vegetables because it's a lot harder to judge a rutabaga when it looks like it's both painfully shy and flirting with you at the same time. My students would always ask, "What's a misunderstood vegetable?" and I'd turn the question back on them: What vegetables do you misunderstand? Of course, it depended on the vegetables my students grew up with. If you grew up in a Japanese or Korean household, you might know daikon radish or Napa cabbage very well (or not), but what about kohlrabi or romanesco? My Indian students usually had no issue with eggplant or okra, but what about rutabaga or radicchio?

I collected slimy okra disaster stories from many white students raised in the North, and tales of overcooked stinky turnips from most everyone regardless of upbringing. Spicy mustard greens and eggplant that turned out either watery or dry often made the list. I interviewed folks: What do you walk right on by and think, yeah, no, I don't know what the hell to do

with *that*? And sometimes it was the pretty squash blossom; the menacing bunch of nettles; the foot-long, slightly hirsute burdock root; and for folks not raised or familiar with Mexican and Central American cuisine, the tomatillo. It turns out that even if you are familiar with some of these vegetables based on your cultural upbringing or where you were raised, you may not know much about them. In other words, it's likely that you may not be all that familiar with a good number of the vegetables described in this book.

But let's back up a bit. I was a picky kid.

I thought tomatoes were evil, exploding, pulp-spewing mutants. I was also a little dramatic. For a kid growing up in New Jersey, hating on tomatoes was an unforgivable hill to die on. Beets were sickly sweet dirt rocks. Eggplants were sluggy, snot-like torture veggies. I didn't grow up with okra, but Lord knows if I did, they'd have some serious explaining to do. I eventually outgrew my pickiness, but hey, it's a process. It required some hand-holding, some trust, and some real skill-transferring. Most of us slowly build up a repertoire with a handful of known and accessible veggies. Throw many of us a carrot or a cup of peas and even non-cooks have ideas. Give a cook a head of cauliflower or a bunch of asparagus and, these days, very few are confused. But the ugly, the twisted, the hard-to-get-to-know types, the finicky—in short: the misunderstood—well, we all need a hand to turn our mistrust and wariness into a functional and loving relationship.

I've made a career out of taking the unapproachable and breaking it down for the novice—first with fish, then with mushrooms, most recently with the science and art of taste and flavor. Nothing pleases me more than witnessing those aha moments when knowledge flows easily from point A to B. When the lifelong eggplant hater turns the corner into eggplant accepter or, dare I say, eggplant lover, I've done my work.

There isn't much of a lobby for some vegetables. No road map to demystify the gnarled root, the twisted tuber, the prickly green. Until now.

What is a misunderstood vegetable? It's pretty simple. As I outlined earlier: If you've walked by a vegetable in the store and you have no idea what the bloody hell to do with it or even what the heck it is, it's misunderstood. If a vegetable is one you've cooked or eaten once or twice and you think the texture is weird, or it's bitter and you don't really like it, then it may have been prepared improperly (and maybe you blamed the cook's failed technique on the vegetable itself). If so, it's likely misunderstood. And

finally, what about those vegetables that you can only think about one or two uses for? When you read the word *tomatillo*, what dishes immediately come to mind? I'll wait here for a moment.

That's right: salsa came to mind, didn't it? And for some of you, maybe you thought: chile verde. (If you grew up cooking tomatillos, insert your own misunderstood vegetable into this example.)

If only one or two dishes come to mind, that's a misunderstood vegetable, too.

It takes more than googly eyes to bring the respect and approachability to these vegetables that they rightly deserve—it takes understanding them for what they truly are. It requires thinking about them in a new way.

Let's keep going for a moment with the tomatillo example. A tomatillo is more than a vehicle for making an awesome salsa (and read more about my favorite one on page 100). At its core, it is a very tart thing, with a texture and acidity level not unlike a green tomato. If you think of a tomatillo as something that can provide a tart component to a dish, you can break it out of its limited box. Instead of vinegar in a salad dressing, you can use a tomatillo and blend it up with olive oil for a vinaigrette. Char them and use them as an alternative to tomatoes in a panzanella salad with grilled peaches and mozzarella (see page 97). Slice them in half, lightly batter them, and continuing with the green tomato theme, turn them into fried green tomatillos (see recipe on page 95).

When you can break down the vegetable into what it provides to the recipe or how it tastes raw (did you know that raw turnip, kohlrabi, and rutabaga are delicious and far more interesting on a vegetable platter than the obvious choices you usually see?), you will never again look at it in the wild and be flummoxed.

It turns out the unfamiliar ones, the dirt-covered ones, even the ones that sting you when eaten raw, hold the best secrets. That celery root and all its "hideous" cohorts are your new best friends. Let's get to know them.

How to Use This Book

I've organized this book by season. For each vegetable, I've included some basics:

- **The 411** gives you a general overview and why I chose to include it; namely, what makes this vegetable "misunderstood"?
- **AKA** lets you know the Latin name for the vegetable and its most well-known common names.
- And then, more obviously, are **the nutrition facts; seasons; purchase, storage, and prep tips; cooking tips; and substitutions.**

Kitchen Glossary

This section is a collection of kitchen terms that describe equipment, techniques, and ingredients that I use throughout the book. It's not exhaustive but hopefully it's useful.

BAKING SHEET: A pan that is 18 by 13 inches is the size of a "half sheet" pan, and that is what I tested these recipes with, using unbleached parchment paper as a liner.

CAST-IRON PAN: I use cast-iron pans for most of my cooking, save for one nonstick egg pan, a stockpot, and a few saucepots. Where I mention using a cast-iron skillet, I'm hoping that your cast iron is seasoned so that you don't encounter sticking problems. If you don't have cast iron, substitute with a heavy-duty skillet, but not a nonstick one unless specified in the recipe, as nonstick pans don't caramelize food very well.

CRISPER DRAWER: Most of your vegetables should be stored in the high-humidity vegetable crisper drawer. The low-humidity setting is for ethylene-producing produce, which tends to be fruits. Keep those separate from your vegetables.

DEGLAZE: This is the process of adding liquid to a pot or pan where stuck-on bits have caramelized, and then scraping these flavorful bits and reintegrating them into the dish or sauce. Conveniently, it's a great way to make your food taste better and cleanup easier.

HIGH-HEAT OIL: This oil is, as implied in the name, for cooking over high heat; it has a higher smoke point. I use safflower oil in my kitchen, but other choices are canola, sunflower, peanut, rice bran, avocado, and many more. Olive oil does not have a smoke point as high as the ones I've named; however, some studies imply that olive oil is also less likely to break down at higher temperatures. I do use olive oil for roasting vegetables with a high heat, and so do most Italians, who have been using olive oil in this fashion for centuries.

OLIVE OIL: Where olive oil is mentioned, I mean extra virgin olive oil. For cooking I use an inexpensive everyday extra virgin olive oil. For finishing a dish or for salad dressings, I use a favorite extra virgin olive oil (I really like Arbequina olive oils).

PRODUCE BAG: There are many kinds of produce bags out there these days besides the single-use plastic bags you get at the store. Mesh-type bags are for carting your produce to and from the store. They are not meant to store your produce, as they will allow too much moisture loss. Your produce will wilt as a result. For storage in the refrigerator, you want a bag that holds some moisture in but that is also breathable. You can find cotton or linen produce bags online that fit the bill. They are a bit pricey, but they are washable and reusable. If you are using plastic bags from the grocery store and you want your produce to hold up in storage, use a fork to poke some small holes in the bag to allow for some ventilation, or leave the top open a bit. Produce needs to breathe a little.

SALT: I use Diamond Crystal Kosher Salt as I find it easy to grab and sprinkle. It is less salty than Morton Salt, and so using Diamond Crystal makes it harder to accidentally over-season food. Cooks have strong opinions on their preferred brand of kosher salt. I'm Diamond Crystal for life! If you use Morton Kosher Salt, use half of what I recommend in the recipes and then taste. You will likely need to add a bit more. I also use flaky salt in my recipes as a finishing salt. You can find Maldon Sea Salt Flakes (from England) at nicer markets or online. You can also find domestic flaky salt (Jacobsen Salt Co. out of Oregon sells a flaky salt).

SEASONED RICE VINEGAR: I use this Japanese ingredient a lot in my cooking. It contains sugar and salt and is very convenient when making quick pickles and salad dressings. Make sure you are buying the correct one, as unseasoned rice vinegar is usually right next to it on the shelf. The brand Marukan is the one I use for these recipes.

VEGETABLE: The term "vegetable" is used generally in this book even if it refers to a bean (fava bean), a fruit (eggplant, tomatillo), or a flower (squash blossoms). Indeed, many of the "vegetables" in this book are not technically vegetables at all.

Spring

Fava Beans

THE 411: Fava beans (as the name implies) are not a vegetable but a legume (like chickpeas) eaten as a vegetable. They are passionately adored all over the world and may have been domesticated as early as the 11th century B.C. The pods contain the fava beans, nestled lovingly on the most velvety soft bed imaginable, as if each bean were a piece of precious jewelry. Fava beans are slightly sweet with a hint of grassiness. They have a lovely, meaty texture. Whereas edamame (soybeans) have this snappy pop to them, fava beans are dense, with a creaminess reminiscent of cannellini beans.

Fava beans, and the riches contained within, are held in the highest esteem in numerous countries, finding their way into dishes that are central to numerous cuisines. In China, Sichuan cuisine relies heavily upon a mixture of favas, soybeans, and chile peppers to make the spicy funky paste known as *doubanjiang*. Egyptians make falafel with favas and not the chickpeas that are common in the Middle Eastern preparation. *Ful medames* is a cooked and mashed fava bean dish with oil, cumin, salt, and sometimes garlic that is a popular Egyptian breakfast food eaten with bread. In Ethiopia, fava beans are extremely popular and used to make a flour called *shiro* and a stew from the flour called *shiro wot*. Italians adore them, especially with Pecorino cheese. In Turkey, they find their way into dips with yogurt and dill and combined with artichokes.

In the United States, however, they are barely used in home kitchens.

Many gardeners in this country know that favas fix nitrogen in the soil and are a great cover crop, but so few of us grow them for food. They can be eaten fresh or dried, raw, lightly cooked, and stewed. The young, tender fava leaves can be deep fried for a garnish, made into a pesto, or thrown on the grill for a short time and eaten with olive oil, salt, and a squeeze of lemon. What's the disconnect, my fellow Americans? Is it the double shelling that puts you off? I get it. It can be a bit labor intensive. Is it the fact that they rarely, if ever, show up at regular supermarkets and you need to go to a natural foods market, farmers' market, or grow them yourself? Quite possibly. Let's start a trend of people in the US demanding fava beans so that they will be easier to find because the whole world can't be wrong.

AKA: *Vicia faba,* broad bean, faba bean, Sichuan bean, orchid bean, silkworm bean.

NUTRITION FACTS: Fava beans, being technically a legume and not a vegetable, contain far less water than typical vegetables (11 percent) and far more protein (26 percent). Fava beans are rich in folate and dietary minerals. Fava beans have the highest protein-to-carb ratio, beating out lentils and chickpeas, among others.

SEASON: Spring is peak fava bean season, though the season can be extended into early to midsummer.

PURCHASE, STORAGE, AND PREP TIPS: Look for green pods that appear bright with no obvious shriveled bits and browning. Give them a squeeze. The pods should feel full and not limp or hollow. Pick pods that are not huge and potentially older unless you plan to dry the beans. Look for medium-sized pods. Also avoid really tiny pods to save yourself the work of shucking the pods to only find two beans inside. Fava beans can live in a produce bag in your crisper drawer for three to five days, though keep in mind they take up a lot of room for the amount of edible product you get (see the accompanying box). Consider shelling the beans out of the pods when you get them home to save precious fridge space. You can cook them the following day.

COOKING TIPS: Once the fava beans are out of their pods, unless they are very young, you're going to need to cook them for at least a few minutes before using them for your recipe. The process involves a quick blanch and cold water shock to remove the second shell off the bean. Bring some salted water to a boil. Meanwhile, grab a bowl and throw in some ice and water. Blanch (boil) the fava beans for one to two minutes (depending on the size), and then shock (chill) in the ice water. Strain them out of the ice water. Locate the little sprout bit where the bean curls inward. Using your thumbnail, peel back that bit and squeeze the outer pod to push out the tender bright green inner bean. With some practice you will soon learn how to shoot them across the room into a bowl. It's great fun. Now the fava beans are ready for your recipe.

SUBS: If you can't find fresh fava beans and you are making a stewed dish, butter beans (lima beans) or cannellini beans are an adequate substitute. For fresher dishes with fava beans where they are served quickly cooked and still bright green, I recommend using frozen edamame or fresh, barely blanched peas.

How Much Fava Do You Get from a Fava Bean Pod?

- You'll need to buy 1 pound (455 grams) of fava bean pods to get roughly 3 ounces (85 grams) of beans ready to use in recipes.
- Because math is fun, I turned that into a ratio, 5:1, where the 5 is the pods, and the 1 is the good stuff.
- Stated another way: If you want 1 pound of fava bean meat, you better bring two baskets to the market because you'll need 5 pounds of fava bean pods.

Spring Soup *with Fava Beans, Tarragon, and Peas*

If you could distill a season into a soup, it would be this one. Full of vibrancy, with a chartreuse hue and oodles of spring vitality, this soup comes together surprisingly fast once the favas are released from their velvet sleeping bags. Using a mixture of spring herbs makes this dish more layered in flavor. If you're fond of tarragon, make sure to include some, as it has a natural affinity for favas and peas.

SERVES 4

1 cup raw cashews

1 cup water

2 teaspoons salt, divided, more if needed

2½ pounds unshelled fresh fava beans, divided

2½ tablespoons olive oil, divided

1 small fennel bulb (about 6 to 8 ounces), small diced, fronds saved if available

1 small onion, small diced

1 bunch scallions, white parts cut in rounds, greens cut in bias and reserved for garnish

½ cup dry white wine or white vermouth

One 12-ounce bag frozen peas

3 cups water

1 cup mixture of picked fresh herb leaves (tarragon, fennel fronds, mint, dill, parsley, basil), divided

2 teaspoons white wine vinegar, divided, more if needed

Freshly ground black pepper, to taste

1 red radish, julienned, for garnish

Combine the cashews and water and let sit for 30 minutes. Add the softened nuts, soaking water, and ½ teaspoon of the salt to a blender and blend on high for 2 to 3 minutes until it's a very smooth, creamy consistency. Transfer to a container and set aside.

Depod the fava beans, blanch, shock with cold water, and peel them. (See fava bean depodding and peeling protocol on page 18.)

In a medium soup pot over medium-high heat, add 2 tablespoons of the olive oil. After a minute, add the fennel bulb, onion, and the white parts of the scallions. Add ½ teaspoon of the salt and sauté until softened, about 7 minutes. Deglaze with the white wine and cook, stirring, for a few more minutes. Add the bag of peas (still frozen is fine) and one-half of the fava beans (reserve the rest for the garnish) along with the 3 cups of water. Bring to a boil, reduce to a simmer, and cook for 10 minutes. Transfer to a blender, add half of the cashew cream (reserving the rest for garnish) and ¾ cup of the herb leaves, and blend until it's a very smooth consistency. Pour back into the soup pot and season with the remaining 1 teaspoon salt, 1 teaspoon of the white wine vinegar, and freshly ground black pepper. Season to taste.

In a small bowl, combine the remaining herbs with the radishes, the other half of the fava beans, the remaining 1½ teaspoons olive oil, and 1 teaspoon vinegar.

Garnish with the radish mixture, scallion greens, and reserved cashew cream.

Fava Beans *with Pecorino, Lemon, and Olive Oil*

This bar snack is straight out of Italy, where so much of the cuisine is built around impeccable ingredients and the wisdom to get out of their way. You'll want to use your favorite olive oil here and some nice flaky Maldon salt (or the equivalent). Don't even slice the bread; rip at it with your hands. Open a chilled bottle of Pinot Bianco, Soave, or Vernaccia and invite some friends over to play a game of Scopa (a really fun Italian card game).

SERVES 4, AS A SNACK

2½ pounds unshelled fresh fava beans
1 lemon, peel cut into thin 1-inch slivers,
    plus 1 tablespoon juice
2 tablespoons of your best olive oil
2 ounces Pecorino Romano cheese, shaved
Flaky salt, for garnish
Rustic bread, for serving

Remove the fava beans from their pods. Blanch, shock with cold water, and peel them. (See fava bean depodding and peeling protocol on page 18.)

Place the fava beans in a shallow bowl, toss with the lemon zest and juice, and drizzle with the olive oil. Lay the Pecorino Romano shavings on top along with a sprinkle of the flaky salt. Serve with the rustic bread and copious amounts of white wine.

Fava Bean, Sweet Pea, and Ricotta Dip
with Spring Vegetables

I recognize that double-shelling fava beans can be some work, so I've supplemented with frozen peas here to limit the preparation time. But please don't hesitate to go all in on the favas if you have the time or free labor. The vibrancy of this dip is stunning—it nearly glows with its chartreuse hue. The dip comes together very quickly once you have the fava beans prepped. I've included a recipe for homemade ricotta on page 48 (because once you've gone homemade, it's hard to go back), but I'm not in your kitchen judging you, so you can totally go buy the ricotta.

SERVES 4

2½ pounds unshelled fresh fava beans

One 10-ounce package frozen sweet peas, thawed (about 2 cups peas)

1 cup homemade Ricotta (page 48; or use store-bought whole milk ricotta)

1½ teaspoons salt, plus more to taste

½ teaspoon freshly ground black pepper

2 tablespoons fresh dill

2 ounces cream cheese

1 lemon, zested and juiced

3 tablespoons olive oil

1 teaspoon white wine vinegar

Assortment of spring vegetables (see Note)

Remove the fava beans from their pods, blanch, shock, and peel them. (See fava bean depodding and peeling protocol on page 18.)

Place the prepared fava beans (save a handful back to garnish the dip), peas, ricotta, salt, pepper, dill, cream cheese, lemon zest and juice, olive oil, and white wine vinegar in a blender jar. Process until creamy. Taste and adjust, as needed. Garnish with the reserved fava beans. Serve with an assortment of spring veggies.

Note

You can use an assortment of spring vegetables for this dish: young radishes, snap peas, tender carrots chopped into bite-sized pieces, or in the case of asparagus, blanched, shocked, and left whole, if you like.

Burdock

AKA
ARCTIUM LAPPA, GREATER BURDOCK, GOBO, EDIBLE BURDOCK, BEGGAR'S BUTTONS, THORNY BURR, HAPPY MAJOR

THE 411: Burdock is a wonderful thing—so nutty, so crunchy, with a texture that is nearly impossible to describe but I'll try: if a twig of your favorite tree was edible and you could walk up to it à la Willy Wonka and just pull tender strips from it and have a tree snack, you'd be on the right track. If you've strolled through a field of random tall weeds and you came home with burrs stuck all over your pants, then you may have come in contact with burdock, a common weed that is the inspiration behind Velcro. On the culinary side, if you've shopped at an Asian supermarket and wondered what that two-foot-long, skinny, hairy parsnip-ish thing was, well you've come to the right place. (If you don't know what a parsnip looks like, head to page 152.) Burdock is considered native to a wide swath of the world, from Scandinavia to Russia to the Middle East to China and Japan. It is mostly consumed in Japan, Korea, and Taiwan, and it has been used as traditional medicine in Japan and China for centuries. Burdock was eaten in Europe in the Middle Ages, but it seems to have been dropped as a vegetable for reasons one can only guess. Perhaps a two-foot-long hirsute root wasn't in fashion any longer.

The flavor of burdock? If artichoke, chestnuts, and sunchokes got in a room and said, "We can do better!" the result would be burdock. And if you're not sure about the flavors of artichoke, chestnuts, and sunchokes, you're probably not alone. Those foods are also often misunderstood. Several cuisines have already figured out how to make burdock something you will want in your life. *Kinpira gobo* (page 27) is a mainstay Japanese preparation, which is exactly how I initially learned about burdock, and I recommend it as your starting point.

AKA: *Arctium lappa*, greater burdock, gobo, edible burdock, beggar's buttons, thorny burr, happy major.

NUTRITION FACTS: Burdock is loaded with fiber, is high in vitamin B_6, magnesium, and potassium, and has an antioxidant profile that blows other vegetables out of the water (field?).

SEASON: Spring is the time to harvest burdock, though it stores well in the ground through winter.

PURCHASE, STORAGE, AND PREP TIPS: Choose slim roots, no more than one inch in diameter. Small and young roots are less fibrous. Make sure there are no cracks and that they are firm. If you can bend them over, they are past their prime. Store burdock in damp paper towels in a sealable bag. Keeping the moisture in this vegetable is key to getting it to last for a few weeks in your crisper drawer. When you are ready to use it, scrub it well. Instead of peeling it, you can use the back of a knife to scrape it, removing any tougher bits of skin. The skin holds a lot of burdock's unique flavor. It oxidizes quickly, so you'll want to have a bowl of water with a splash of vinegar or lemon halves in there. Let the burdock pieces soak in the acidulated water as you cut them (unless you are going to be browning them in the dish anyway). If the earthy, strong flavor of burdock is not your thing, soaking shredded or thinly cut burdock in that acidulated water mellows the flavor, taking some of the funk away. And if you like burdock but it's still a bit strong for you, go ahead and peel it.

COOKING TIPS: Burdock can be tough, so make sure to cook it thoroughly until it gets tender. It takes a bit longer than you might think. To give it a head start, I tend to add it to a dish when I cook the onions at the beginning of a preparation. I also cut burdock into smaller pieces if I know it's not going to simmer in a liquid.

SUBS: It would be hard to replace the unique texture of burdock, but sunchoke would get you there with its nutty flavor. Other possible substitutes: lotus root, parsley root, celery root, or carrot.

Kinpira Gobo (Braised Burdock and Carrot)

Kinpira gobo is a traditional Japanese salad, and it was my personal gateway into all things burdock. Burdock oxidizes quickly when you cut it, but you don't need to worry in the slightest about that here because the tamari will change the color anyway, masking the discoloration. This salad holds up beautifully for several days, so feel free to double the recipe and enjoy those leftovers. You'll need to plan ahead if you want to use the homemade shiitake dashi, as it infuses overnight. Instant dashi is an option, though it contains fish flakes.

SERVES 4

½ pound burdock (*gobo*), peeled (or scraped as described on page 25)

1 tablespoon plus 2 teaspoons toasted sesame oil, divided

1 large carrot, julienned

1 teaspoon red chile flakes

1 cup shiitake dashi (recipe follows)

2 tablespoons gluten-free tamari (or soy sauce)

2 tablespoons sake

1 tablespoon sugar

2 tablespoons mirin

1 teaspoon toasted sesame seeds

Cut the burdock into julienne or use a sharp knife and shave off thin slices as if you were whittling a stick, which you are sort of doing (see my reference to burdock as being the most delicious twig ever on page 25).

Heat a large sauté pan over medium-high heat. Add 1 tablespoon of the sesame oil. Add the burdock and cook, stirring, for 3 to 4 minutes. Add the carrot and chile flakes and sauté for another 1 to 2 minutes. Add the dashi, tamari, sake, sugar, and mirin. Continue to cook, stirring occasionally until the mixture is glazed and no liquid remains. Turn off the heat, stir in the final 2 teaspoons of toasted sesame oil and toasted sesame seeds. Eat warm, at room temperature, or cold. All temperatures are delicious with this salad.

continues ➡

SHIITAKE DASHI

*Dashi normally contains fish flakes (*katsuobushi*), but you can make a great vegetarian version with this recipe. The overnight cold infusion does all the work for you. Use instant dashi for a fast substitute; note: it contains fish.*

MAKES ABOUT 3½ CUPS

4 cups water
15 grams (½ ounce) kombu
10 dried shiitake mushrooms

Pour the water over the kombu and mushrooms. Allow it to sit overnight in the refrigerator. The next day, strain through a fine-mesh strainer. Dashi can be stored in the fridge for up to a week or in the freezer for 2 to 3 months. The spent kombu can be sliced thin and used in salads. The shiitakes can be repurposed, sliced, and sautéed and used in another dish (I typically remove the stems, as they are often tough).

Fried Rice *with Burdock, Sesame, and Seaweed*

Fried rice is not a food, it's a lifestyle. It's also one of the best ways to use up leftovers. Pro tip when ordering Thai or Chinese takeout: order extra rice specifically to make fried rice the next day. It's much easier to make fried rice with cold, day-old rice than with hot, fresh rice, as fresh rice is a bit too wet to get good caramelization going. You may not be familiar with dulse, one of the most delicious sea vegetables you can eat. It's available in most natural foods markets or online. Look for the Maine Coast Sea Vegetables brand. The burdock root adds a lovely earthy, nutty flavor with a hint of sweetness. The pickled burdock is an important brightening garnish, contrasting the richness of the rice and highlighting burdock in two different, complementary ways.

SERVES 4 TO 6

½ pound burdock root, peeled (or scraped as described on page 25), divided

¼ cup seasoned rice vinegar

¼ cup high-heat oil, divided

4 cups cooked white rice (jasmine or other medium-grain rice; see Note)

1 small onion, minced

1 medium carrot, small diced

1½ ounces ginger, grated

2 eggs

½ ounce dulse flakes

2 tablespoons gluten-free tamari (or soy sauce)

1 tablespoon toasted sesame oil

Salt, to taste

Hot sauce, Spicy Chile Oil (page 188) or chile flakes, to taste

Cut half the burdock into very small dice and peel the other half with a vegetable peeler into 4- to 5-inch strips. Take the burdock strips and add them to the rice vinegar and set aside to quick pickle.

Heat a wok or large skillet over high heat and add 1 tablespoon of the oil. When the oil is just beginning to smoke, add half of the rice and cook, tossing frequently until the rice is light brown in places and broken up into individual grains, about 3 minutes. Remove the rice to a bowl and repeat with another tablespoon of oil and the rest of the rice. When the second batch of rice is done, add the first batch back in and scrape all the rice up the sides of the wok or pan, leaving the middle free. Add another tablespoon of oil and stir-fry the onion and diced burdock in the center of the wok or pan for 3 to 4 minutes. Add the carrot and ginger to the middle and stir-fry for another 2 to

continues ➤

3 minutes until all the veg is tender. Push the vegetables up the side of the wok or pan, once again leaving a hole in the middle. Add the final tablespoon of oil.

Mix up the eggs with a fork and then quickly scramble them. Mix all the ingredients together, along with the dulse, tamari, sesame oil, salt, and hot sauce, plus 2 teaspoons of the rice vinegar from the pickling burdock root. Transfer the fried rice to a serving dish or individual bowls.

Strain the burdock strips out of the rice vinegar and garnish the fried rice with curls of the burdock. Taste, adjust the seasoning, and serve.

Note

If you don't have leftover rice, but still want to make the dish, there is a work-around. Cook up a pot of fresh rice, fluff it, and then spread it out on a sheet pan and cool it for a few hours in the fridge. Then proceed with the directions in the recipe.

Burdock and Miso Soup

Red miso packs a similar punch of flavor to burdock, which is exactly why they are paired up in this dish. The optional inari can be found in Japanese markets in packets or purchased online. You'll need to plan ahead if you want to use the homemade shiitake dashi, as it infuses overnight. Instant dashi is an option, though it contains fish flakes. If you end up enjoying this version of miso soup, I recommend making a big batch of the shiitake dashi and freezing it in quart-sized containers. Next time you're craving miso soup, simply add the block of frozen dashi to a pot along with the burdock and tamari. Simmer the mixture on the stovetop and a deeply nutritious and satisfying soup will be yours in 30 minutes.

SERVES 4

1 tablespoon dried wakame

¼ cup cold water

4 cups Shiitake Dashi (page 28)

1 teaspoon gluten-free tamari (or soy sauce)

½ pound burdock root, scraped, cut into ½-inch rounds

¼ teaspoon salt

1 tablespoon toasted sesame oil

¼ cup red miso

7 ounces soft tofu, cubed

4 inari (fried tofu pouches), sliced into thin ribbons, for garnish (optional)

1 tablespoon toasted white sesame seeds, for garnish (optional)

A few chives, cut on the angle into thin slices, for garnish (optional)

In a small bowl, add the wakame to the cold water and allow to rehydrate, about 5 to 10 minutes. When it's soft, squeeze out the water and set the wakame aside. Discard the water. The wakame is now ready to use.

In a soup pot over high heat, add the shiitake dashi, tamari, burdock, and salt and bring to a boil. Reduce to a simmer and gently cook for at least 30 minutes until the burdock is tender. Add the sesame oil to the soup. Ladle out 1 cup of the soup into a bowl and whisk the miso into the soup until it's smooth. Turn the heat off the soup and pour the miso-soup mixture back into the pot. Ladle the soup out into four bowls and garnish each bowl with tofu, wakame, and the optional garnishes.

nettles

AKA

URTICA DIOICA, STINGING NETTLE, COMMON NETTLE, BURN NETTLE, NETTLE LEAF, STINGER.

THE 411: If you're up for adventure, nettles are something to check off on your culinary badass list, especially if you harvest them yourself. After all, "stinging" is baked into the name, making this one of only a handful of foods to offer a soupçon of fear along with dinner. So, if this is your first time cooking stinging nettles, give yourself a well-deserved pat on the back. Allow me to walk you through the experience, my gloved hand in yours.

Native to western North Africa and temperate regions of Asia and Europe, nettles can now be found worldwide. They grow especially well in moist climates, making the Pacific Northwest stinging nettle central. To wit, I know a restaurant and a farm in the PNW with "nettle" in the name. Nettles are supremely tasty, somewhere between spinach and green tea. And they are so packed with nutrients they make kale look like junk food. But to get to the goodness, you must respect the plant. The sting in stinging nettles comes when you brush up against tiny hairs on the leaves or stem, resulting in a cocktail of pain, welts, and tingling (a form of contact dermatitis). Gloves are a required bit of protection when handling them. Drying or cooking nettles defeats this nasty defense, rendering nettles as innocent as a bunch of lettuce. But until that point, they pack a fierce wallop to which few are immune. (Once, when harvesting nettles, my dog ran through a field of them, and I can confirm that even dogs with thick coats will dance around in pain just the same way humans do when they inadvertently walk through a nettle patch wearing shorts, or so I've heard.)

The uses for nettles are many, and not all of them are confined to the cooking pot. Indigenous Americans traditionally cooked the plants in spring, when they are young, tender, and less sting-y; and later in the growing season, they harvested the fibrous stems for use as fishing line. Nettles are tools, food, tea, and medicine, and a grand harbinger of spring. And also, apparently, they are food fodder for silly and painful competition, as the thousands of people drawn to the county of Dorset in the United Kingdom can verify at their annual World Nettle Eating Championship. If you have to ask why, you might not have what it takes to be a contestant.

AKA: *Urtica dioica*, stinging nettle, common nettle, burn nettle, nettle leaf, stinger.

NUTRITION FACTS: Nettles are extremely high in calcium and protein (blowing kale out of the water), rich in vitamin A (kale edges out nettles on this one), and a good source of fiber.

SEASON: Early spring is the peak time to harvest nettles for cooking. There is another less robust season in early fall.

PURCHASE, STORAGE, AND PREP TIPS: It's difficult to find nettles in the marketplace. The only places I've seen them sold—very occasionally in the spring—is at natural food markets. If you live in an area with a robust farmers' market, you may see them sold there. In Seattle, we are lucky enough to have several foragers represented at our farmers' markets and can buy them there in season. If you are not in a place where they are sold, you are left with the only option: find a local patch and harvest them early in the season, typically in March through May. Luckily, they seem to grow in most temperate parts of the country. If you're not sure where they grow near you, simply ask around. Someone has most likely been accidentally introduced to a patch and has a story to tell. See the box on page 37 for more information on how to pick them.

It's best to use nettles as soon as you can, before they wilt and lose their fresh vibrancy. However, if you must store them, place them in a paper bag (make sure they are dry) and store them on a shelf in your refrigerator. Moisture on the nettles will lead to deterioration. The paper bag helps keep them dry and allows for air circulation. In fact, nettles are so high in protein that moisture leads to spoilage. If you'd like to dry them to use for tea, make sure to keep the stems separate from one another so that there is good air circulation.

To prep nettles, get a large pot of water going. I like to blanch and shock them the same way I do fava beans, except I blanch the nettles for longer, for a total time of seven minutes. While I use salt in nearly all my blanching pots for vegetables, for nettles I don't because I want to use the steeping liquid for other purposes and don't want it to be salty. This liquid is a lovely tonic, and it's one of the healthiest teas you can drink or use in your cooking. I freeze it and use it in soups, green smoothies, and anywhere a rich, grassy, green flavor is welcome.

A long pair of tongs is your friend here. Once the nettles go into the boiling water, press them down with the tongs so that all the plant material is submerged. Once blanched for seven minutes, pull the nettles out of the boiling water and place them into a bowl of ice water to quickly chill and stop the cooking. Drain the nettles through a colander and then squeeze out all of the water. If, when you are doing this, you notice a mild sting on your hands, back into the boiling water they go. This is extremely unlikely if you've cooked them for the required time. Once all the water is squeezed out, you can rough chop them, young stems and all, and proceed to use them in recipes.

COOKING TIPS: Cooking nettles, once they are prepped (blanched and shocked, drained

How to Forage for Nettles

1. Grab a basket or several large grocery store paper bags, gloves, a long-sleeved shirt, and a pair of scissors.
2. Make sure the nettles you pick are young (early spring), less than 2 feet tall, and not flowering.
3. Make sure you are harvesting nettles! Refer to the photo on page 34 and watch videos online before you head out for the first time.
4. Cut or twist off the top 6 to 12 inches of young nettles; give them a shake to dislodge any twigs, dirt, bugs, or other non-nettle material; and place them in your bag or basket. Many people eat only the leaves and discard the stems. But if you collect nettles when they are young and their stems are bendable, tender, and skinny (¼ inch or less), you can also eat the stems (think of them as you would spinach stems, which you should also eat). Also, picking nettle leaves off stems is a royal pain. I always make sure to pick young nettles and eat the stems.
5. The equivalent of two lightly filled large grocery store paper bags will give you enough nettles for two to three recipes' worth of food. When I make nettle pesto I need one bagful to make a pint of pesto.

and squeezed out), is as easy as chopping them up and adding them to any recipes you would spinach, kale, beet greens, chard, and the like. Because the flavor is so unique, I tend to feature nettles without combining them with a lot of other greens so as to really appreciate how special they are.

SUBS: Spinach mixed with a little ground green tea.

Creamy Scrambled Eggs *with Nettle Pesto*

There is no better way to highlight the deep green flavor of nettles than by setting them off with perfectly creamy scrambled eggs. Definitely consider doubling or tripling the nettle pesto recipe if you've pulled in a haul, as it freezes beautifully. You can freeze the pesto in ¼-cup portions, which makes them ready to go for your next scramble. For a quick primer on perfect scrambled eggs, head to beckyselengut.com.

SERVES 2 TO 4, MAKES ¾ CUP PESTO

FOR THE NETTLE PESTO

1 cup cooked and squeezed nettles (from ½ pound raw; see procedure on page 36)
¾ cup olive oil
2 ounces Parmesan cheese, grated (¾ cup)
½ cup toasted slivered or sliced almonds
½ teaspoon salt, plus more to taste
¼ teaspoon chile flakes (optional)
1 garlic clove, minced

FOR THE EGGS

8 large eggs
½ teaspoon salt
2 tablespoons unsalted butter
2 to 4 slices of toast

TO MAKE THE PESTO

Add all the nettle pesto ingredients to a blender or food processor and blend until well combined. I like a pretty creamy consistency, but you can leave it more textured. Choose your own adventure on this.

TO MAKE THE EGGS

In a medium bowl, whisk the eggs with the salt. Heat a large nonstick pan over medium-high heat. Add the butter, let it bubble, then reduce the heat to medium. Pour in the beaten eggs, grab a rubber spatula, and start stirring. Keep stirring the eggs over a medium temperature, making sure nothing sticks to the bottom. Use the spatula to go around the outside of the pan and then make passes through the middle to keep the eggs evenly cooking. If you do this consistently, you'll have the creamiest, most delicious scrambled eggs you've ever had. Here's the trick, though; you *have* to remove them from the heat when they are still wet and just barely set. Off the heat, they will continue to cook. Once off the heat, stir in ¼ cup of the nettle pesto immediately. Taste and add more pesto and/or salt according to your preference. Serve right away with toast.

Seared Halloumi Cheese *with Honey, Pickled Peppers, and Creamy Nettle Dressing*

Based loosely on a green goddess dressing with its creamy texture and herbal notes, this version brings nettles' foresty, green notes to the mix. Halloumi is a Cypriot goat's and sheep's milk cheese that takes to grilling or searing like a champ. It's salty (no need to season it first), firm, and squeaks playfully between your teeth as you eat it. Pickled chile peppers are terrific in this dish; Mama Lil's is an excellent store-bought choice. If you happen to find them in your grocery store, grab a jar and, according to your spice tolerance, garnish the dish with a few; they're fantastic.

SERVES 4, AS AN APPETIZER

FOR THE NETTLE DRESSING

1 cup whole-fat plain yogurt

1 cup prepped nettles (from ½ pound raw; see procedure on page 36)

¼ cup parsley

3 tablespoons olive oil

1 tablespoon chopped fresh dill

1 tablespoon lemon juice

1 teaspoon gluten-free tamari sauce (or soy sauce)

½ teaspoon salt

⅛ teaspoon freshly ground black pepper

FOR THE HALLOUMI

2 tablespoons olive oil

Two 8.8-ounce packages halloumi cheese, cut horizontally in half to create 4 equal slabs

2 tablespoons honey

1 lemon, cut in half

¼ cup jarred pickled chile peppers (such as Mama Lil's; optional)

TO MAKE THE DRESSING

Blend all the ingredients together using a blender or immersion blender. Taste and adjust, if needed.

TO MAKE THE HALLOUMI

Heat a large skillet over high heat. Turn it down to medium-high. Add the oil and then the halloumi and allow it to brown, about 2 to 3 minutes. Flip and brown the other side.

To serve, spoon the nettle dressing onto a platter. Top with the cheese, shingling them if you like. Drizzle the honey over the top; squeeze the lemon over the top. Garnish with the optional pickled chiles.

Nettle Colcannon *with Potatoes, Cabbage, and Butter*

Colcannon ("white-headed cabbage") is a traditional Irish dish typically made with cabbage or kale. In my opinion, it is one of the topmost divine comfort foods of the world. It might seem like this recipe calls for a lot of butter, and it sort of does. On a whim, I added nettles to the version I usually make. It was a great success, and I'll never make it any other way.

SERVES 4 TO 6

- **2 pounds Yukon Gold potatoes, peeled and cut in half**
- **2 tablespoons salt plus 2 teaspoons, divided, more if needed**
- **1 stick (8 tablespoons) plus 2 tablespoons unsalted butter, divided**
- **½ onion, small diced**
- **1 pound green cabbage (about ½ of a medium one), small diced**
- **½ pound cooked nettles (see procedure on page 36), finely chopped**
- **1 teaspoon freshly ground black pepper, more if needed**
- **2 cups cream**

Add the potatoes to a pot, cover with water, and add 2 tablespoons of the salt. Bring to a boil and then simmer until the potatoes are tender and a knife slips in easily, about 15 to 20 minutes.

Meanwhile, heat a large sauté pan over medium heat. Add the stick of butter and, when melted, add the onion and the 2 teaspoons of salt. Sauté for 5 minutes, stirring occasionally until the onion starts to soften. Add the cabbage and nettles, stir, cover the pot, and let the vegetables soften and cook, checking and mixing them occasionally. In about 10 to 15 minutes, just about when the potatoes are done, add the pepper and cream to the vegetables. Drain the potatoes, add them to the sauté pan of vegetables, and use a potato masher to mash them up. Stir everything together and taste! Add more salt or pepper if you'd like. Serve, topped with 2 tablespoons of butter, because 1 tablespoon is for quitters. Now go tuck into a bowl of comfort. You've earned it.

Radicchio

AKA
CICHORIUM INTYBUS
VAR. FOLIOSUM,
ITALIAN CHICORY

THE 411: Radicchio is a member of the chicory family. Its many varieties and ability to be grown early in the spring necessitated its own chapter. The other chicories are explored in the Winter chapter.

Radicchio hit America in the 1980s at a time when Northern Italian cuisine was all the rage. Balsamic vinegars spiked in usage, a fortuitous thing, as the sweetness and acidity of balsamic balances the sharp bitterness of radicchio. (Also, the super popular "French" dressing of the 1980s just wouldn't taste as good on radicchio.) However, while balsamic vinegar is now in the majority of Americans' lexicon, if not their kitchens, only a small minority recognize radicchio beyond "that red thing in the bagged salad mixes." Compare that to its homeland, where it has been grown and revered for over six centuries. Its primary calling card, a sharp bitterness, is highly appreciated. There are numerous varieties, named for the regions where they originated. In fact, radicchios in Italy are protected by what is known as the Indicazione Geografica Protetta (or IGP, in English: Protected Geographical Indication). Only plants grown in the stated geographical region can be labeled as such. Radicchio, along with many other revered Italian ingredients (prosciutto, Parmesan cheese, wine, and so forth) are protected in this way to help preserve the quality, consistency, and cultural importance of these agricultural products.

Radicchio is misunderstood in America because it is not typically a vegetable that can be eaten on its own unless it is prepared correctly. Not many folks, hardcore Italians aside, can munch on a leaf of raw radicchio the way one might be able to with romaine or arugula. Once you know how to work with it, radicchio holds secret charms and boatloads of nutrition.

Let's Get to Know the Most Commonly Available Varieties of Radicchio, Shall We?

CHIOGGIA

- Most widely available in the United States
- Globe-shaped, deep red
- Created in the early 1900s

TREVISO

- Full name is Radicchio Rosso di Treviso
- Long, ovoid shape
- More pronounced white veins

CASTELFRANCO

- Round heads, yellow-green leaves dotted with red and purple spots and veins
- Inner central head is the prime part of the vegetable
- Sweeter and milder than other types of radicchio

AKA: *Cichorium intybus* var. *foliosum,* Italian chicory.

NUTRITION FACTS: Considered an antioxidant-rich "superfood," you can get more than a day's worth of vitamin K in just five leaves. Radicchio has high amounts of zinc, potassium, and folate.

SEASON: Radicchio is a cool-season plant that can be sowed weeks before the last frost in early spring. It also grows well in the fall and into the winter. Certain varieties can be harvested during the summer, as well.

PURCHASE, STORAGE, AND PREP TIPS: When choosing Chioggia radicchio, look for firm heads, tightly compacted leaves, and vibrant coloring. Treviso should also be firm and vibrant with no obvious browning or soft spots. Castelfranco should look oh-my-god gorgeous with no obvious browning or wilting.

Store all types of radicchio in produce bags in the crisper drawer of the fridge for up to one week. Wash only before you use it to avoid moisture-related mold issues. To prep radicchio, trim the stem and remove any outer leaves if they are wilted. For use in salads, cut the core out and chop the leaves into chiffonade (ribbons) or bite-sized pieces. If you remove the outer leaves and the radicchio is tightly compacted, you need only to give the outside a quick rinse. Much of the bitterness is in water-soluble molecules that are released when it is cut or chewed. If you really can't stomach the bitterness but still want to use radicchio for its color and nutritional benefits, submerge thin ribbons of it in a 30-minute water soak. This will help tame its bitterness.

For those who don't mind the bitterness but want to use it effectively, the key is in matching and balancing the bitterness by using a few strategic techniques. By bulking up your recipes with sweet-leaning ingredients (think romaine lettuce, fruits, balsamic glaze, and the like) and using a fair amount of creamy or fatty ingredients (cheese, nuts, and so forth), the bitterness is suddenly not just tolerable but desirable. Like a dash of bitters in a cocktail, it makes everything more complex, interesting, and balanced.

COOKING TIPS: Grilling or roasting radicchios, especially the firm Chioggia and Treviso types, adds complexity to the vegetable, and the boost of sweetness from the caramelization of sugars adds interest and balance. That being said, you want to avoid burning or aggressively charring preparations, as that can impart its own bitterness.

SUBS: Any of the other members of the vast chicory family would be a good substitute for radicchio, so reach for escarole, Belgian endive, frisée, and the like.

Radicchio Insalata Mista

I learned how to make a version of this salad over 20 years ago when I cooked at Osteria la Spiga in Seattle, a Northern Italian restaurant specializing in handmade pastas and piadina *(a thin flatbread from the Emilia-Romagna region). Co-owned by general manager Pietro Borghesi and chef Sabrina Tinsley, the restaurant is operating, as of this writing, in its 25th year. Sabrina has been a mentor to me and countless others. She is a tireless advocate for young chefs, women in the restaurant world, our local culinary college, and BIPOC chefs, founding a Future of Diversity Guest Chef Program. So, yes, this is a great salad, but, to me and many others, it's so much more than a salad. La Spiga is a must-stop if you visit Seattle.*

SERVES 4

½ teaspoon salt, more if needed

¼ teaspoon freshly ground black pepper, more if needed

1 teaspoon sugar or honey

½ cup white wine vinegar (my favorite producer is Castello di Volpaia)

1 cup olive oil

1 small head Chioggia radicchio (or medium head of Treviso or Castelfranco), cut into bite-sized pieces

1 large head romaine lettuce, cut into bite-sized pieces

4 cups baby arugula

1 large carrot, peeled into ribbons

In a medium bowl, whisk the salt, pepper, and sugar into the white wine vinegar until the salt and sugar dissolve. Whisk in the oil slowly to combine. Season with salt and pepper to taste. Set the dressing aside.

Combine the radicchio, romaine, arugula, and carrot ribbons in a large bowl. Pour half of the dressing over the top (you'll have leftover dressing for another day). Toss gently with your hands. Add more dressing if it needs it. It should be nice and tart. Season to taste with more salt. Serve.

Sourdough Toasts *with Charred Radicchio, Walnut Mint Pesto, and Ricotta*

This recipe is in the top five of my favorite recipes in this book. There's something special about the crunch of the toast, the bite of that radicchio, the creamy ricotta, and the herbal nutty notes of the pesto. Feel free to cut the finished toasts into small pieces and serve this as an appetizer. Or keep the toasts whole and serve this with Spring Soup with Fava Beans, Tarragon, and Peas (page 19) for a lunch or light dinner. You can use any leftover ricotta from this recipe to make Abby's Most Beautiful Beet Salad in the World (page 113), or you can use it in Fava Bean, Sweet Pea, and Ricotta Dip with Spring Vegetables (page 22).

SERVES 4

FOR THE WALNUT MINT PESTO
¾ cup walnuts
½ cup mint leaves
¼ cup olive oil
¼ teaspoon salt
1 garlic clove, minced fine
⅛ teaspoon red chile flakes

FOR ASSEMBLY
3 tablespoons olive oil, divided
10 ounces Chioggia or Treviso radicchio (1 medium head), cores removed, cut into bite-sized pieces
1 teaspoon salt
2 tablespoons balsamic vinegar
1 tablespoon brown sugar
8 slices sourdough bread, cut ¾ inch thick
8 ounces Ricotta (recipe follows for homemade or use store-bought whole milk ricotta)
2 tablespoons honey
2 tablespoons of your favorite olive oil

Preheat the oven to 350°F.

Spread the walnuts out on a baking sheet and toast until lightly browned, 8 to 10 minutes. Set aside to cool. To make the walnut-mint pesto, put all the pesto ingredients into a food processor (or you can use an immersion blender for this) and pulse to a slightly chunky texture. Taste and adjust as needed. Set aside.

To prepare the radicchio, heat a large skillet over high heat. Add 1 tablespoon of the olive oil. Add the radicchio and salt, stir once, and then let it sit in contact with the pan to caramelize. Stir occasionally. If your pan is too small, do this in two batches. When the radicchio has wilted and some parts have browned a bit, add the balsamic and brown sugar. Keep stirring until all the liquid has evaporated. Take off the heat.

Turn on the broiler. Place the pieces of bread on the baking sheet and drizzle with

continues ➤

2 tablespoons of the olive oil. Broil on the middle rack, watching the bread carefully so it doesn't burn. You want it to be browned and crispy on top. Remove from the oven and set aside.

To put it all together, spread an equal amount of ricotta on each toast. Spoon about 1 to 2 tablespoons of pesto on top of the ricotta, spreading it out. Top with the radicchio. Finish with a light drizzle of honey and your favorite olive oil on top.

RICOTTA

MAKES 2 CUPS

3¼ cups whole milk, not ultra-pasteurized
¾ cup heavy cream, not ultra-pasteurized
1 cup cultured buttermilk
Salt, to taste

Combine the milk, heavy cream, and buttermilk in a large pot and cook over medium heat, stirring occasionally. Once the mixture has reached 180°F, stop stirring. When the mixture forms curds and the whey separates and becomes clear, turn off the heat. Let it sit off the heat for 30 minutes, undisturbed, to allow the curds to strengthen.

Set a strainer over a bowl and line with two layers of cheesecloth. Pour the ricotta onto the cheesecloth and let it drain until most of the whey is out. I typically do this in the fridge, as it can take about 30 minutes to fully drain. But you can certainly leave the ricotta with more moisture if you want to do a quicker drain.

Salt to taste (usually about ¾ teaspoon). Fresh ricotta will last in your fridge for about 1 week.

Warm Radicchio Salad *with Salsa Verde, White Beans, and Smoked Salt*

This is one of those handful of this, handful of that dishes. Leftover beans? Check. Stale bread? Perfect. Some leftover parsley and a bunch of pantry ingredients? Check. Buy some radicchio and you're ready. The salsa verde has umami, salt, acid, sweetness, fat, and the bite of chiles; the croutons add texture; the radicchio adds bitterness; and the parsley, rosemary, and smoked salt bring in aromatics. Each ingredient plays its role here, none more important than another, to create layers of flavor and texture in a salad that's humble in nature but more than the sum of its parts.

SERVES 4

FOR THE SALAD

1 cup dried white beans (or two 14-ounce cans of drained cooked beans)

1½ teaspoons salt, divided

5 to 6 slices stale hearty bread, medium diced

3 tablespoons olive oil, divided

¼ cup chopped shallot

1 teaspoon rosemary, fresh, finely chopped

1 head radicchio, cut into bite-sized pieces

1 teaspoon brown sugar

½ teaspoon smoked salt, to taste (or regular salt)

¼ teaspoon freshly ground black pepper, to taste

FOR THE SALSA VERDE

½ cup olive oil

½ cup fresh Italian parsley, roughly chopped

2 tablespoons sherry vinegar

1 tablespoon toasted almonds

1½ teaspoons golden raisins (or currants)

1 teaspoon liquid aminos (or 2 small salted, jarred anchovies)

1 teaspoon capers, rinsed

½ teaspoon sea salt

¼ teaspoon red chile flakes

TO MAKE THE SALAD

Preheat oven to 400°F. Line a baking sheet with parchment paper.

If you're using dried beans, add them to a medium pot of fresh water (enough water to cover the beans by 4 inches) with 1 teaspoon of salt. Bring to a boil and cook for 1 to 2 hours, until tender (see Note). Cool in cooking liquid.

Add the bread cubes to the lined baking sheet. Toss with 2 tablespoons of the olive oil. Sprinkle ½ teaspoon salt evenly over the top. Bake for 10 to 15 minutes, until lightly browned and crisp. Set aside.

Heat the remaining 1 tablespoon olive oil in a medium sauté pan over medium-high heat. Add the shallots and cook for 5 minutes, or until tender. Add the rosemary, radicchio, brown sugar, smoked salt, and pepper to taste and cook until the radicchio starts to lightly brown around the edges, 5 to 7 minutes. Do this in two pans or in two batches, dividing the other ingredients as needed.

continues ➡

TO MAKE THE SALSA VERDE

Add all the ingredients to a blender and blend to a smooth puree, stopping to scrape down the blender several times, as needed.

TO ASSEMBLE

In a large bowl, mix the drained beans with the radicchio and croutons and dress with half of the salsa verde. Taste and see if you'd like more. Serve the salad with any extra salsa verde on the side.

Note

Many sources, including my personal go-to, Serious Eats, claim that you no longer need to soak your dried beans to get a good result, and I concur after many years living the soak-free lifestyle. The beans might, in fact, have more flavor, as you are cooking them in salted water versus soaking them in unsalted water. If you have a pressure cooker, simply cover the rinsed, dried beans with at least 4 inches of water, add 1 teaspoon of salt per cup of dried beans, and you have delicious cooked beans within the hour. Follow your pressure cooker recommendation for timing.

Artichoke

AKA

CYNARA CARDUNCULUS
VAR. SCOLYMUS, GLOBE ARTICHOKE,
FRENCH ARTICHOKE, GREEN
ARTICHOKE, CARCIOFO

THE 411: Let's go with $500 in the category of "Foods that were discovered by ridiculously hungry and persistent people." Answer: "A vegetable that is technically the bud of an undeveloped flower in the thistle family that contains only approximately 25 percent edible matter buried deep in the heart of all the pokeyness." The correct hypothetical *Jeopardy!* question is: "What are artichokes?"

A domesticated variety of wild cardoon, artichokes are native to the Mediterranean. In Europe, the main producers are Italy, Spain, and France. In the Americas, it's Argentina, Peru, and the United States. California provides 100 percent of the US crop, and 80 percent of that is grown in Monterey County, where the town of Castroville proclaims itself the "Artichoke Center of the World."

There should be little controversy in stating that artichokes have been misunderstood, especially in the preparation of fresh ones. They literally have "choke" in the name, which refers to the inedible part at the center that can, well, choke you. Next to "stinging" nettles (see page 34), arti-"chokes" ask us to contemplate personal harm for some scant calories when the world is awash with alternatives that include fast-food burgers. It's an uphill marketing battle! So you may ask: How do you safely eat them, and also why? Deliciousness, my friend! Utter and complete deliciousness. Fresh and clean, slightly nutty, sort of a love child of sunchokes and celery root (with a hint of asparagus) and something else entirely ethereal, artichokes are worth the work of understanding them. Luckily for those not interested in the labor to access them, there are excellent frozen, canned, and jarred versions. And thankfully so, as it takes six fresh artichokes to yield enough hearts to fill an 8-ounce jar—and that's after you remove three-quarters of it as waste. This shouldn't dissuade you from cooking a fresh artichoke because I dare say it's one of the sexiest vegetables/flower pods you'll ever eat. Cook and feed an artichoke to someone you love. Trust me on this one. If the recipes in this section lead to a marriage proposal, email me!

AKA: *Cynara cardunculus* var. *scolymus*, globe artichoke, French artichoke, green artichoke, *carciofo* (Italian).

NUTRITION FACTS: High in fiber, folate, vitamin K, magnesium, and potassium (a similar amount as in a banana).

SEASON: Peak season is in the spring and, to a smaller degree, again in the fall.

How to Prep a Fresh Artichoke

To acidulate or not to acidulate: To keep artichokes from browning while preparing them, many folks recommend filling a bowl with water and squeezing lemons into the water, then storing the artichokes in this acidulated water. Some recommend directly rubbing half of a lemon on the cut parts of the artichoke as you work. I find that this preservation is only necessary if you are going to be serving the artichoke raw, cut into thin slices for use in pastas or salads. For the steaming and roasting recipes, the negligible amount of browning will not be noticed or detected in the final dish.

Removing the top of the artichoke and the pokey tops of the leaves: Using a serrated knife, cut off the top tough 1 inch of the artichoke. Then, using scissors, cut the top ½ inch off the pokey part of the leaves. When you're finished, they should look like the photo on page 59.

Exposing the edible stem: Using a paring knife or Y-peeler, carefully trim or peel the stem of the artichoke. A best practice is to cut off the very end and then peel back the tough outer portion of the stem, preserving the tender inner stem.

Trimming the tougher outer leaves: If you plan to steam or roast the artichoke so that you can scrape the meat off with your teeth, you don't need to spend much time removing tough leaves because the inner part of the leaves is what you're after. Where there is a will, your teeth will find the way. However, if you want to prepare the artichoke down to the heart and the innermost tender leaves, you'll need to carefully peel back all the outer tougher leaves and then use a paring knife to trim away any dark green parts of the artichoke. That is where a bowl of acidulated water comes in handy, as explained above. You can watch me prepare an artichoke at beckyselengut.com.

When to remove the inedible choke: Using a serrated knife, cut the artichokes in half. Leave the inner hairy choke as is for steaming (it's easy to remove after steaming). For roasting, use a spoon or paring knife to carefully cut the furry choke out of each half, including the spiky purple ones. The innermost yellow leaves are the most tender. Be careful as you do this because those spiky leaves can be quite sharp.

PURCHASE, STORAGE, AND PREP TIPS:
Fresh artichokes should be heavy, with the leaves tightly packed together. Fresh specimens will actually squeak if you squeeze them. Some brown streaking on the leaves is fine (supposedly a result of frost). Store them in bags in the fridge for up to five days, though it's recommended to cook them soon after buying them for the best results. It is a (pre)flower, after all.

COOKING TIPS: There are all sorts of ways to cook fresh artichokes, from steaming to roasting to grilling. I would stick with steaming over boiling to preserve more of the nutrients. That said, roasting is my personal favorite way to enjoy them. I also like steaming them until they are close to being done and then finishing them on the grill to impart some smokiness.

SUBS: There is really no great substitute for the experience of eating a fresh, cooked artichoke, but you can get some of the flavor and texture of an artichoke with sunchokes, celery root, asparagus, chayote, and hearts of palm.

Creamy Artichoke and Miso Dip

The best part of this recipe isn't the simplicity of grabbing most of the ingredients from your pantry, nor is it the mild, sweet, and umami-rich take on the humble canned artichoke, it's the chance to explore so many misunderstood vegetables in one go. Serve this dip at your next gathering, surrounded with a party platter of veggie love the likes of which few have seen before. Depending on the season, reach for kohlrabi, rutabaga and jicama sticks, watermelon radish and fennel wedges, daikon radish half circles, purple cabbage leaves, thin sunchoke rounds, and endive leaves.

SERVES 4

One 12-ounce jar or can artichokes (can be whole or quartered, unmarinated), drained

2 tablespoons red miso

2 tablespoons nutritional yeast

2 tablespoons olive oil, more if needed

1 to 2 tablespoons water

¼ teaspoon salt, more if needed

Couple shakes of Tabasco or hot sauce of your choice

Freshly ground black pepper, to taste

Squeeze of fresh lemon juice, to taste

Selection of raw misunderstood vegetables for dipping

Put everything but the dipping vegetables into a blender and puree to a creamy consistency for at least 2 minutes at high speed. Add a bit more olive oil if you need it to get the blender to puree properly. Taste and adjust the salt, lemon juice, pepper, and/or hot sauce to your taste. Serve right away or pop in the fridge for up to a week.

Artichokes *with Preserved Lemon Butter and Parsley Bread Crumbs*

I'll never forget my first artichoke, steamed and served with melted butter. A revelation in its simplicity, the flavor like nothing I'd had before—grassy, slightly sweet, a little bit of earth and mineral, slight nuttiness, and then of course the butter, licked off my fingers after scraping every bit of goodness from the leaves. I remember, in my artichoke high, leaving behind a scattered pile of plant detritus like the aftermath of a crow picking through a compost pile. As the comedian Margaret Cho famously said, it's time "to put on (your) eating dress." And maybe a bib, 'cause it's gonna get buttery up in here.

SERVES 4

FOR THE PRESERVED LEMON BUTTER (SEE NOTE)
1 stick (8 tablespoons) unsalted butter, softened
1 tablespoon minced preserved lemon peel
1½ tablespoons lemon juice (from 1 lemon)
1½ teaspoons champagne vinegar
1 small garlic clove, minced
½ teaspoon flaky salt, to taste

FOR THE PARSLEY BREAD CRUMBS
1 tablespoon preserved lemon butter
1 cup panko
½ cup parsley leaves, divided
Salt, to taste

FOR THE ARTICHOKES
4 globe artichokes

FOR THE GARNISHES
1 lemon, cut into ¼-inch wheels
¼ cup chive blossoms (optional)

TO MAKE THE PRESERVED LEMON BUTTER
Add the softened butter to a food processor and combine with the lemon peel, lemon juice, vinegar, garlic, and salt. Taste for seasoning.

TO MAKE THE PARSLEY BREAD CRUMBS
Melt 1 tablespoon of the preserved lemon butter in a small skillet over medium-high heat. Add the panko and cook until it absorbs the butter and crisps, about 3 minutes. Finely mince half of the parsley and mix into the panko just before serving the dish. Season with salt. You'll use the other parsley leaves to garnish the dish.

TO PREPARE THE ARTICHOKES
Prep the artichoke as explained on page 54. For this preparation you'll be cutting them in half but leaving the thistly chokes in until after they are done steaming. Fill the bottom

continues ➤

of a steamer with water. Bring to a boil. Add the artichoke halves to the steamer insert. Turn the heat to medium-low. Cover the pot and set a timer for 15 minutes. To check for doneness, insert a knife into the heart; if the knife comes out easily, they are done. Or if the uppermost leaves pull out of the artichoke easily, they are done. Let the artichokes cool and then use a spoon to scoop out the hairy chokes. Refer to the photo on page 59 to see what it should look like when the choke is removed.

PUTTING IT ALL TOGETHER

Sprinkle the parsley bread crumbs all over the artichokes (you can even tuck some in between the leaves). Garnish with the whole parsley leaves, lemon wheels and optional chive blossoms, and serve with ramekins of melted preserved lemon butter.

Note

Feel free to double the preserved lemon butter to tuck some away in the freezer for another time. Shape it into a log on some parchment paper, roll it up, pop it into a freezer bag, and freeze it. Then simply slice off medallions of the butter as you need it in future dishes.

Heather's Oven-Roasted Chokes *with Creamy Dijon Mustard Sauce*

"There is nothing," I used to think, "better than a steamed artichoke with butter." I thought wrong. It's a roasted artichoke, the edges of the leaves curled and crunchy, nutty and caramelized in the oven, the heart sweet and yielding, dipped in a piquant, creamy sauce (but butter would also be divine).

SERVES 4

FOR THE ARTICHOKES

4 tablespoons olive oil

2 whole globe artichokes, leaf tips cut with scissors (optional; see method in box on page 54), top ½ inch cut off with a serrated knife, stem trimmed, cut in half vertically, choke scraped out with a spoon

1 lemon, zested (zest and 2 tablespoons juice reserved for sauce), the rest cut into 4 chunks

FOR THE CREAMY DIJON MUSTARD SAUCE

½ cup mayonnaise (or yogurt)

2 heaping tablespoons Dijon mustard

2 tablespoons lemon juice

Zest of 1 lemon

½ teaspoon black pepper, more if needed

TO MAKE THE ARTICHOKES

Preheat the oven to 400°F. Line a baking sheet with parchment paper. Drizzle the olive oil on the artichokes and use your hands to coat them well. Tuck a quarter of the already-zested lemon under each artichoke. Roast the artichokes, loosely covered with foil, for 45 minutes to 1 hour, until you can easily remove an outer leaf from the artichoke.

TO MAKE THE MUSTARD SAUCE

While the artichokes are roasting, grab a medium bowl and make the mustard sauce. Whisk together the mayonnaise with the rest of the sauce ingredients. Season to your taste, adding more pepper or mustard—it should be highly seasoned. Keep cold.

Serve each person an artichoke with some of the sauce.

summer

eggplant

THE 411: Eggplant is a "nightshade" vegetable, related to chiles, potatoes, and tomatoes (tobacco, as well). The origin of the term *nightshade* is largely unknown, some saying it is because plants in that family prefer growing in shade and bloom at night (though this certainly doesn't apply to heat-loving eggplants, chiles, and tomatoes). The family of vegetables has been associated, anecdotally, with inflammation. Confusingly, the much-lauded Mediterranean diet is full of nightshade vegetables. My advice: if it doesn't seem to be causing you any issues, include them in your diet for their many benefits, deliciousness being primary in my mind.

China and India are the leading producers of eggplant, and if you like eggplant, look to these cuisines for inspiration in ways to use them. There is little agreement concerning where eggplant originated, whether it comes from India, China, Africa, or South Asia. There appears to be no ancient Greek or Roman names for eggplant, yet there are numerous Arabic and North African names.

Eggplant is misunderstood right from the get-go: Why is it called an "egg" plant? Does it taste like an egg? (Answer: no.) There are many types of eggplants, and the name was coined in reference to a small, round, white cultivar that resembled an egg. We don't see that variety very often in the marketplace, leading to some confusion with the name. What we tend to see in stores are the large, deeply purple, nearly black "globe" eggplants, which can be cooked in a variety of ways. The Italian eggplant is more dense, a bit smaller, and a bit more flavorful than the globes. Japanese eggplants are long and slight, dark purple in color, and make a great choice when you want a fast-cooking eggplant. Chinese eggplants can be longer than the Japanese variety and have a pretty light-purple color. And finally, we have Thai eggplants, which are small and green with a firm, crisp texture. These are best cooked lightly, unlike the other varieties that need longer cooking times. There are several more varieties you may see at farmers' markets, some long and bulbous

There appears to be only a few possible human responses when queried as to the likability of eggplant:

1. **Lovers:** Oh it's divine, isn't it? It's really my favorite vegetable! Such an exceptional flavor! So creamy and rich and meaty.
2. **Haters:** Like a slug making love to a worm on my dinner plate. Vile. Loathsome.

There is no middle ground. Said no one: I don't really have an opinion on eggplants.

and white, others purple and striped, all fairly similar in texture inside but beautiful in their diverse color palette.

Beyond the confusion with the name, there are other reasons the eggplant is misunderstood, and nearly all of it comes down to the texture and improper cooking techniques. A few cooking tips are all you need to level up your eggplant cooking game.

AKA: *Solanum melongena,* aubergine (United Kingdom and Ireland).

Is It Necessary to Pre-Salt Eggplant to Remove "Bitterness"?

Many recipes instruct readers to salt eggplant slices, let them sit for 30 minutes or longer, rinse them, and pat them dry before cooking to "remove the bitterness." There *is* a slight bitterness to eggplant that diminishes in the cooking process, though some supertasters who are more sensitive to bitterness may never fully come around to loving eggplant. But long gone are the days of cultivars that had a notable bitterness. These days, farmers prefer growing eggplants that are sweeter and less bitter, making the step of pre-salting them to remove "bitterness" unnecessary. But wait, before you stop pre-salting them: eggplants are mostly water, and so this step is beneficial for other reasons. Most notably, it draws out some of this water, softening the pieces in the process, which then leads to a more even and faster cooking process. Another benefit to pre-salting is that you are brining the eggplant, which creates an evenness of flavor throughout. It makes a difference. So, don't feel like you have to salt the eggplant ahead of time in order to have good results. But if you want great results, I'm on team pre-salt.

Here's how to do it:

1. Cut the eggplant into slices. Sprinkle salt evenly over the top (you need only sprinkle salt on one side).
2. Let it sit for about 30 minutes or so. You will see moisture beading up on the surface.
3. If you are serving the eggplant with salty ingredients (soy sauce, cheese, olives, capers, and the like), go ahead and put the slices in a colander and give them a quick rinse before spreading them out on a towel and gently rolling the towel to dry the slices. You could also sandwich the slices between two towels and gently press down. You can skip the rinsing step if you're not concerned about the dish getting too salty and simply proceed to pressing the slices to remove any moisture.

You're ready to cook!

NUTRITION FACTS: Eggplant is high in fiber, manganese, and antioxidants.

SEASON: Peak season is late summer, and that's when you'll get the best flavor. However, eggplants are available year-round in most markets.

PURCHASE, STORAGE, AND PREP TIPS: For all types of eggplants, choose ones that are shiny and firm, with no divots or obvious soft spots. Avoid any that appear shriveled or dried out. Don't buy the biggest eggplants in the store, as bigger is not necessarily better. You may find that bigger eggplants are less dense, and the big ones certainly take longer to cook if you are cooking them whole (as, say, in the Smoky Baba Ghanoush with Garlic and Za'atar on page 68). Store eggplants in a bag in your crisper drawer and use them within three to five days. I have never once felt the need to peel an eggplant. Some do this because they don't like the texture of the peel. If, after following the advice for properly cooking eggplant, you still have an issue with the texture or flavor of the peel, by all means peel it. There are many small seeds in an eggplant, but they are edible and, when cooked, soften to the extent that they are nearly undetectable.

COOKING TIPS: Due to the high water content of eggplants (80 to 90 percent), it's especially important that you give them plenty of room as they cook. Equally as important is making sure the heat is high enough to quickly evaporate that moisture. While you can steam eggplant, it's not my favorite way to cook it, as I find you miss out on the extremely complex flavor of the eggplant when dry heat is applied to it. There's a reason you've probably rarely seen "steamed eggplant" on a menu. Eggplant needs to be fully cooked to be delicious, and this is often where people go wrong. While I'd love to give you an exact time for doneness, there are too many variables (what variety, what size, what type of heat, how close to the heat source, and so forth). Instead, look for signs of doneness to know when the eggplant is cooked. It should be caramelized, aromatic, tender, and almost wet looking in the middle without any white or light patches of undercooked flesh. If you've ever had an eggplant that had a dry, cottony texture to it, it was most likely undercooked.

SUBS: There's no great substitute for the complex, earthy, rich, mildly bitter (in the best way) flavor of eggplant, but portobello mushrooms come the closest with their umami-rich, earthy flavor profile. Some sources suggest summer squash as a substitute, but frankly that would disappoint me (I'm not a squash hater, by any means, but that substitute might get you partway there in texture but nowhere close in flavor).

Smoky Baba Ghanoush *with Garlic and Za'atar*

If you've been making hummus for years as your go-to Middle Eastern dip, it's high time to diversify your repertoire. The secret to the best baba ghanoush is to make sure the eggplant is in contact with high heat and plenty of smoke (preferably wood smoke) so that it can be properly charred. If you don't have access to fire and wood smoke, in a pinch you can also use your oven's broiler, though you won't get the smokiness unless you combine broiling with a smoky ingredient, such as smoked salt, or use a smoking gun (which is super fun, so you might consider it). You need to cook the eggplant past where you think you should. It should be charred all over and limp. It will look sad and wrong, but it's not. Once the eggplant is scraped out of the skin, give it a merry-go-round tour of your salad spinner (or dry it very well in an absorbent towel) to release extra moisture and concentrate the flavors of the smoky eggplant. I've included a recipe for the spice mix called za'atar because fresh is always best. But these days you can find za'atar spice blends in many specialty markets.

SERVES 4

FOR THE BABA GHANOUSH

3 pounds globe or Italian eggplant

1 package of pita bread

1 large garlic clove, minced and smashed with the side of a knife into a paste, more if needed

2 lemons, juiced, more if needed

2 teaspoons salt, plus more to taste (use smoked salt if you are not grilling or smoking)

2 tablespoons tahini (I like tahini made by Soom, which you can get online)

½ cup olive oil (use your highest quality one), more if needed

FOR THE ZA'ATAR GARNISH (OPTIONAL)

¼ cup sumac

2 tablespoons dried thyme

2 tablespoons dried oregano

1 tablespoon toasted sesame seeds

1 teaspoon salt

TO MAKE THE BABA GHANOUSH

If grilling: Turn your grill on high heat. Poke some holes in the eggplant with the tines of a fork. Cover the grill and cook the eggplant on one side until it's charred, 8 to 10 minutes. Flip the eggplant over and repeat on the other side. Cook until it's charred and the eggplant is limp. While the grill is still hot, throw the pita on there to char it lightly on both sides. Wrap it in foil to keep it warm.

If broiling: Preheat the broiler. Poke some holes in the eggplant with the tines of a fork. Broil on the top rack until it's charred (it typically takes about 7 to 10 minutes per side, but ovens vary, so check on it every few minutes). Flip the eggplants over and repeat on the other side. Cook until it's fully charred and the eggplant is limp. It's totally OK if the eggplant skin is papery and the flesh has exploded out of the skin a bit.

Let it cool for a bit and scoop the soft flesh out of the peel. If a little peel stays on, don't worry about it! Dry the eggplant flesh in a salad spinner or with a towel. If you've used your broiler, consider adding smoked salt to the finished dish to impart some smokiness. Or use a smoking gun with the nozzle inserted into the bowl of scooped-out eggplant, covered tightly with foil, according to manufacturer's directions.

Put the eggplant in a medium bowl along with the garlic, lemon juice, and salt. Using a fork, beat it up well. Be aggressive—it helps to break down the eggplant fibers and also whips it up to add lightness and creaminess. Add the tahini and continue beating. Secure the bottom of the bowl on the counter with a slightly damp towel so you can use the fork with one hand, and drizzle the oil with the other. Slowly drizzle the olive oil in as you are mixing with your fork. You are trying to emulsify the fat into the eggplant so that it has a nice homogenous texture. Now it's time to taste and adjust with more lemon, garlic, salt, and olive oil, according to your palate.

TO MAKE THE ZA'ATAR

For the optional za'atar garnish, mix all the ingredients together in a bowl. Transfer to an airtight container. Keep in mind that when you sprinkle the za'atar garnish over the top, you'll be adding more salt to the mix.

Serve with the warm pita for dipping. (If you've broiled your eggplant, rewarm the pita, wrapped in foil, in a 400°F oven, or quickly heat it in a skillet on both sides.)

Grilled Eggplant *with Tomatoes, Pomegranate, Spiced Yogurt, and Pine Nuts*

This is a riff on an Afghan recipe I learned how to make over 20 years ago called borani banjan, *which features fried eggplant stewed in tomatoes. It's a dish that has its roots in Persia, but versions of it are eaten all over the world. This version is a bit lighter, as you are grilling the eggplant instead of frying it and using fresh versus stewed tomatoes. In addition to the pine nuts that add contrasting texture to the eggplant, a garnish of fried chickpeas (available in small bags as a snack in most supermarkets) gets sprinkled on top. Black garlic adds a rich, deep, savory-sweet note to the yogurt sauce. This is a dish to make in late summer, when heirloom tomatoes and eggplants are at their peak.*

SERVES 4

FOR THE EGGPLANT
1½ teaspoons salt
1½ pounds eggplant, cut into ½-inch slices
½ cup olive oil

FOR THE YOGURT SAUCE
1 cup full-fat yogurt
½ head black garlic cloves (mashed into a paste if hand mixing sauce), or 2 regular garlic cloves, minced well
1 tablespoon olive oil
1 teaspoon ground cumin
½ teaspoon salt, more if needed

FOR THE GARNISH
Flaky salt, to taste
1 pound heirloom tomatoes, cut into ½-inch slices
1 cup cherry tomatoes, cut in half
¼ cup toasted pine nuts
½ cup basil, roughly torn
Pomegranate molasses, as needed
1 tablespoon mint, roughly chopped
1 small bag of crunchy chickpeas (optional)
Good olive oil, as needed

TO MAKE THE EGGPLANT
Pre-salt the eggplant as explained (see box on page 66). If grilling: toss the eggplant in the oil, then grill over high heat until caramelized and tender, 6 to 8 minutes. If pan-searing: add the oil to a pan and cook the eggplant over medium-high heat until caramelized and tender, 6 to 8 minutes. (You could also coat with oil and roast in a 400°F oven until caramelized.)

TO MAKE THE YOGURT SAUCE
Puree all the ingredients in a blender or mix well by hand. Season to taste.

TO ASSEMBLE
Salt the tomatoes to your taste. On a large platter, spread out the yogurt sauce. Shingle the eggplant with the tomatoes on top. Garnish with the cherry tomatoes, pine nuts, basil, some pomegranate molasses, mint, chickpeas, and good olive oil. Serve at room temperature.

Eggplant Parmesan *with Mint and Basil*

Eggplant is one of my favorite foods, full stop. My wife, April, despises it. In our marriage alone, you see proof of the only two possible ways humans can feel about this controversial vegetable (see the box on page 65). So when it comes to sneaking my favorite foods past the food critic in my home, I have to be sneaky. April will eat eggplant Parmesan, and she especially likes this version. My theory is that the pre-salting (see box on page 66) masks some of the bitterness she detects (did I mention she's a supertaster?). Plus add enough cheese and tomatoes, and even the pickiest eater will be sufficiently ~~manipulated~~ distracted into loving your favorite foods.

SERVES 6 TO 8

Salt, as needed

2 pounds globe or Italian eggplant, cut into ½-inch slices

High-heat oil for frying, as needed

3 eggs

1 tablespoon milk

1 cup flour

3 cups homemade tomato sauce or one 25.5-ounce jar tomato and basil sauce (I like Muir Glen)

1 pound fresh mozzarella (sold in logs, sliced or whole, or in large balls)

¼ cup chopped fresh mint

¼ cup chopped fresh basil

4 ounces grated Parmigiano-Reggiano

Preheat the oven to 375°F.

Pre-salt the eggplant as instructed in the box on page 66.

Heat a few wide sauté pans over medium-high heat and add 2 tablespoons of oil to each pan. Once the oil is shimmering, add a few slices of the eggplant at a time, cooking both sides until golden, 1 to 2 minutes per side. Remove them and place on a paper towel. When done frying all the eggplant slices, remove them from the pan and set aside. You may need to do additional batches depending on how big your pans are. Eggplant sucks up a lot of oil, so you'll need to wipe out the pans each time to remove browned bits, then bring to medium-high heat between each batch.

Once the slices have been cooked the first time, you'll bread and refry them. To do so, add ¼ cup of oil to each pan. Heat on medium-high until a little piece of the breading sizzles. In a small bowl, whisk the eggs and milk. Set up two shallow bowls: one with the flour and another with the beaten eggs and milk. Coat each eggplant slice generously with flour. Tap off the excess and then dip into the egg and milk mixture. Cook briefly until golden on both sides, about 1 minute per side (they will brown quite quickly, so keep an eye on them). Place them onto a paper towel–lined plate.

To assemble, lightly coat the bottom of a 9-by-13-inch casserole dish with tomato sauce and place one layer of eggplant on top. Slice the mozzarella into ¼-inch slices and top the eggplant with half the cheese. Sprinkle half of the chopped mint and basil on top of the mozzarella. Top with more sauce, sprinkle with half of the grated cheese, and repeat the process, finishing with tomato sauce and the remainder of the grated cheese.

Pop the casserole into the oven and bake, uncovered, for 30 to 40 minutes, until the cheese melts and the top is browned up nicely and bubbling.

Okra

AKA

ABELMOSCHUS ESCULENTUS,
OCHRO, OKRO, GUMBO,
LADIES' FINGERS

THE 411: And we have arrived at the most misunderstood vegetable (historically, culturally, and culinarily). Okra is a flowering plant in the mallow family, the same family marshmallows originally came from. Its origin is debated. Some say it's from West Africa or Ethiopia, others say it originated in Southeast or South Asia. What we do know is that ships carrying enslaved Africans brought okra to America; it is a storied food that cannot be separated from the complex and brutal way it arrived on our shores. The oft-repeated story of okra, millet, rice, and other seeds being braided into the hair of African children crossing the Atlantic on slave ships is metaphorical, part of an oral history weaving a connection between the home Africans were taken from, the land that African slaves were forced to work, and the many generations that have come since. Despite, or perhaps because of, the complex history inextricably linked to okra, it has become a staple and comfort food in the South, as well as in urban areas populated by Black Americans who moved out of the South during the Great Migration. In his celebrated book *The Cooking Gene,* Michael Twitty writes, "In mainland North America, okra was one of the ultimate symbols of the establishment of the enslaved community as a culinary outpost of West Africa." Dr. Jessica Harris, author of *High on the Hog: A Culinary Journey from Africa to America* (who prefers her okra stewed), told me that "wherever okra points its green tip, Africa has been. This is not just in the United States or the Western Hemisphere but worldwide."

For more information:
- Read the book *High on the Hog: A Culinary Journey from Africa to America* by Dr. Jessica B. Harris and then watch the Netflix series.
- Watch Michael Twitty make okra soup on YouTube and then follow him on his site: afroculinaria.com.

As for the culinary reasons I included okra in a book called *Misunderstood Vegetables,* we'll just let the slime out of the bag on that one. I admit, the first time I had okra, I was put off by the exuberant ectoplasm and considered the need for a culinary exorcism. It was my first time cooking it, and I didn't know what I was doing. People who are unfamiliar with okra misunderstand it because they don't know how to use its mucilaginous nature to their benefit to create thickness, body, and texture in stewed foods or in gumbos. Or they don't know the tips and tricks to get rid of it should okra jelly not be their jam. I have provided one recipe in this chapter that makes use of this "magic" gel (see page 80 for Southern-Style Stewed Okra and Tomatoes) and two that use high heat to dry it out.

I have grown to love okra for its grassy, vegetal flavor, for its complicated but fascinating history, and even for the rich gel that thickens stews.

AKA: *Abelmoschus esculentus*, ochro, okro, gumbo, ladies' fingers.

NUTRITION FACTS: Okra is high in fiber, vitamin C, vitamin B$_6$, calcium, and magnesium.

SEASON: Summer and into early fall.

PURCHASE, STORAGE, AND PREP TIPS: Choose brightly colored okra pods that are smooth with no obvious brown spots. There will be some browning where the pod was taken from the plant, which is fine. Many people swear by picking okra that is no longer than your pinky, as it can get tough as it gets larger (though a long stewing in a gumbo would make it perfectly edible and tender). For quick-cooking dishes that aren't stewed, choose the smaller ones. Store okra in a produce bag in your crisper drawer, but use it as soon as possible. They are no longer good if they are soft or have gone brown. Don't wash okra pods until you are ready to use them to avoid moisture-related mold issues. Dry them well after washing them (the gel from the cut okra will combine with any clinging water and you'll have a stickier mess on your hands). To prep okra, simply cut off the very tip of the pod where it was connected to the plant.

COOKING TIPS: You'll find many ideas out there for how to "deal" with okra. Everything from drying it out overnight, to soaking it in a vinegar solution prior to rinsing and cooking (so as to reduce the mucilage by breaking it up and dissolving it), to cooking it whole to keep the slime from coming out (pro tip: it's still in there). I have found that there are three things that really help to reduce the gel texture: heat, air, and acid. High heat, as in pan or deep frying, grilling, or high-heat oven roasting, reduces the water content significantly, which firms up the offending gel (if it offends you). Good air circulation dries out okra, and when cooking with high heat, simply avoid piling pieces of okra on top of each other to prevent steaming: the more liquid that is present allows for the mucilage to dissolve in the water, creating the sticky goo that many don't prefer. Cooking with acidity brightens any okra dish and also seems to mitigate the goo. Personally, I don't do any vinegar soaks or overnight drying out, but I do use high heat, provide good air circulation, and cook or pair okra with acidic ingredients. Or I embrace the gel in stews and gumbos and let it do its thing. I find that in stew form, the gel is a welcome addition.

SUBS: Cactus paddles (nopales) have a similar grassy flavor and mucilaginous texture. Eggplant, zucchini, and green beans, while different, certainly, come closest to replacing okra in recipes where it is not the main ingredient.

Radha's Okra Bites

My neighbor and friend Radha loves okra as much as I do, and I reached out to her for her favorite way to eat it. She sticks to a gluten-free, mostly vegan diet, and I've been experimenting with alternative flours and dairy sources recently. Could I make a pan-fried okra dish accessible to most diets that tasted just as good as what you might typically get from a restaurant when you order fried okra? There was only one way to answer that question, so on went the stove. I served up batch after batch of okra to my jury of tasters. I'd call it a glorious success, but I'll let you be the judge and jury. I prefer to eat these on their own with just a squeeze of lemon juice, but feel free to serve it with Comeback Sauce (page 95). If you want to keep this okra recipe vegan, however, sub out the yogurt and mayo in the sauce recipe for coconut yogurt and vegan mayo.

SERVES 4

1 cup coconut or almond yogurt
  (or cow's milk yogurt)
1 pound okra, trimmed, cut into
  ½-inch pieces
1 cup coconut flour
½ cup oat or almond flour
½ cup fine cornmeal
2 teaspoons salt
¼ teaspoon cayenne pepper
4 cups high-heat oil
Flaky salt, for garnish
1 lemon

Add the yogurt to a medium bowl. If the yogurt is very thick, add a tablespoon of water to thin it out just a bit. Add the okra to the bowl with the yogurt and mix well. Add the flours, cornmeal, salt, and cayenne pepper to a paper bag. Transfer the yogurt-coated okra pieces to the paper bag and shake the bag with some enthusiasm. Transfer the coated okra pieces to a parchment-lined baking sheet.

Heat the oil in a large cast-iron skillet or saucepan to 350°F.

Line another baking sheet with paper towels. Fry the okra in batches until very crispy, about 3 to 5 minutes. To confirm, take one out and, after it cools for a moment, feel it with your finger. If it feels soft, keep the batch frying for a bit longer. Remove the okra from the oil with a fine mesh strainer and transfer to the paper towel–lined baking sheet. Sprinkle immediately with some flaky salt.

Serve right away, with a squeeze of lemon.

RADHA'S OKRA BITES
(PAGE 77)

SOUTHERN-STYLE STEWED
OKRA AND TOMATOES
(PAGE 80)

Southern-Style Stewed Okra and Tomatoes

Ask most Southerners to tell you about their thoughts on okra and you'll need to get comfortable because there will be stories. Southerners love their okra, whether it is stewed with tomatoes as in this classic take or in gumbo or pickled and peeking out of a Bloody Mary or deep fried. Even though I'm a Yankee from New Jersey, my many friends from the South have made me an okra convert. My good friend Brian Medford hails from North Carolina, and this recipe is an adaptation of one that he has made his whole life. He's a Yankee now (at least according to his ZIP code), having moved to Astoria, Oregon, where he owns the Rusty Cup, a sweet little café in one of my favorite towns. But he'll always be a Southerner at heart—as well as a talented pastry chef, educator, and okra ambassador. Y'all look him up if you find yourself in Astoria.

SERVES 4

½ stick (4 tablespoons) unsalted butter

1 sweet onion, small diced

1 jalapeño pepper, seeded and small diced (cut a few rounds of jalapeño and set aside for use as an optional garnish)

1 teaspoon salt, plus more to taste

½ teaspoon smoked paprika

⅛ teaspoon chipotle chile powder (optional)

1 pound okra, trimmed, cut into ½-inch rounds

2 garlic cloves, finely chopped

2 pounds fresh tomatoes (8 cups, medium diced) or 8 cups canned tomatoes

½ cup vegetable stock or water

6 cups cooked rice, to serve with stew

Trappey's peppers in vinegar (optional)

Tabasco or Crystal hot sauce (optional)

Heat the butter in a large saucepan over medium-high heat. Add the onion, jalapeño, and salt and cook until the onion starts to brown, about 10 minutes. Add the smoked paprika and chipotle chile, if using. Add the okra, turn the heat to high, spread the okra out, and lightly brown it, stirring occasionally, for about 5 minutes. Add the garlic and stir everything together, then add the tomatoes and stock. Bring the mixture to a boil, reduce to a low simmer, cover, and set a timer for 20 minutes.

Adjust the seasoning and serve over hot rice with the vinegar from the bottle of Trappey's peppers and hot sauce, if using. Garnish with the reserved jalapeño rounds, if using.

Sesame-Roasted Crispy Okra
with Peanut Sauce and Tomato-Corn Salsa

In a nod to okra's West African heritage, I've combined high-heat roasted okra with a rich peanut sauce and a bright salsa with in-season corn and tomatoes. Plantain chips (plantains are also a West African staple food) get broken up and combined with sesame and peanuts as a textural contrast. The peanut sauce will last in your fridge for a week or two. Any leftover crunchy garnish can be kept in an airtight container at room temperature and used to add texture to salads or as a topper for soups or stews.

SERVES 8

FOR THE OKRA
2 pounds okra, ends trimmed, okra left whole
¼ cup olive oil
1 tablespoon sesame oil
1 teaspoon salt
¼ cup white rice flour

FOR THE PEANUT SAUCE
½ cup creamy peanut butter
¼ cup water
2 tablespoons lime juice
1 tablespoon gluten-free tamari (or soy sauce)
1 teaspoon liquid aminos (or fish sauce)
1 teaspoon honey
Salt, to taste

FOR THE TOMATO-CORN SALSA
1 cup cherry tomatoes, cut in half
1 ear of corn, kernels cut off
¼ cup chopped cilantro
1 lime, zested and juiced
2 tablespoons olive oil
Salt, to taste

FOR THE CRUNCHY GARNISH
2 ounces plantain chips, broken up
2 tablespoons toasted peanuts
2 tablespoons toasted black sesame seeds

TO ROAST THE OKRA
Preheat the oven to 450°F. Toss the okra in the olive and sesame oils. Salt the okra and then toss in the rice flour. Lay out on a cooling rack over a cookie sheet and roast until the okra is browned in places and crispy, about 30 to 40 minutes. Check halfway through for doneness.

TO MAKE THE PEANUT SAUCE
Puree all the ingredients together in a blender. Set the sauce aside.

TO MAKE THE SALSA
In a medium bowl, mix all the salsa ingredients together and set aside.

TO MAKE THE CRUNCHY GARNISH
In a medium bowl, mix all the ingredients and set aside.

TO PUT THE DISH TOGETHER
Spread the peanut sauce out on a platter. Top with the salsa. Then lay out the okra on top of that and garnish with the crunchy things.

Squash Blossoms

AKA
CUCURBITA SPECIES,
CUCURBITA PEPO, ZUCCHINI
BLOSSOMS, ZUCCHINI FLOWERS,
SQUASH FLOWERS, COURGETTE
BLOSSOMS

THE 411: Squash blossoms, as the name might suggest, are not a vegetable but a flower. Squash blossoms come from the *Cucurbita* species, which also includes zucchini, yellow summer squash, spaghetti squash, and many other types of squashes and pumpkins. All the blossoms from these vegetables are edible, and all can be used in your cooking. In fact, the photo on page 82 comes from pumpkins, not squash at all. They can be in all shades of yellow and orange and are as beautiful as they are tasty. They are mild in flavor, reminiscent of the squash or pumpkin they come from, lightly sweet, with a melt-in-your-mouth quality when cooked and slightly peppery and bright when raw.

Squash blossoms have a long history of use in Mexico, Turkey, Italy, Greece, Spain, and the Middle East. They have become more popular in the United States as farm-to-table cooking has become part of our culinary fabric. You are unlikely to find squash blossoms in many stores, although every now and again you will see them in specialty markets. The place to source squash blossoms in the summer months are at farmers'

markets and in either your garden or the garden of a friend who's trying to foist a ginormous zucchini on you. Kindly thank them for the offer and ask, instead, if you might go and harvest all of the female zucchini blossoms. A win-win for everyone (harvesting the female flowers means no more ginormous zucchini and you get your blossoms to use in these recipes). If you want to keep growing zucchini, harvest the male blossoms (they have longer stems).

AKA: *Cucurbita* species, especially *Cucurbita pepo,* zucchini blossoms, zucchini flowers, squash flowers, courgette blossoms.

NUTRITION FACTS: Let's be real here: you'd have to eat a truckload of squash blossoms to get much nutrition out of them. You're eating them because they are beautiful and delicious and not for their nutritional qualities, which are there but in very, very tiny amounts.

SEASON: Summer is peak season, though you will see some in the spring and into the fall in milder climates.

PURCHASE, STORAGE, AND PREP TIPS: Squash blossoms are super delicate so, if possible, you should pick them or buy them the day you use them, ideally in the morning before the heat of the sun wilts the leaves. Look for bright blossoms that have no wilted or bug-eaten petals. Choose the biggest ones you can find, as it makes it easier to remove the pistils and stamen and you get more petals for less work. To store petals you will use that day, simply put the stems in a glass of water as you would any bouquet of flowers. For overnight storage (and I don't recommend you store this delicacy for more than overnight), you can lay them out (unwashed) on paper towels and cover them with more paper towels (to absorb any moisture that might be along for the ride) and store them on a rack in your fridge. Squash blossoms can be dirty or buggy. Due to their delicacy, I recommend washing them only if you can see some little critters inside that are also enjoying the beauty of your harvest. If so, you can either step outside and shake loose the little critters or very gently swirl them around in some cool water to dislodge the hangers-on. Gently transfer them to a towel to let them dry before proceeding with next steps. The entire squash blossom is edible, though many prefer to remove the stem and pistil or stamen (pistil in females, stamen in males). Some say the pistil or stamen can be bitter, but I haven't noticed that. I remove the pistil and stamen because I can fit more filling in there when I'm stuffing them. Try it with and without removing them and let your palate be your guide. For cooking the blossoms, I like to leave some of the stem attached because I think it makes for a nicer presentation,

---

How to Prepare a Squash Blossom for Its Big Day on Your Plate

1. Clean the blossom if necessary.
2. Carefully open the blossom to reveal the stamens (for male flowers) or the pistils (for female flowers).
3. Using your fingers, scissors, or tweezers, remove the stamens or pistils from where they attach at the base of the flower. It is sometimes easier to do this by gently tearing the blossom down one side and laying it flattish like an open book for better access. If you are stuffing the blossom, this also makes it easier to get the filling exactly where you want it, which is at the base of the flower.
4. For stuffing the blossom, use a piping bag, plastic bag with a corner snipped off, or a teaspoon. Fold the petal over where you stuffed it and twist up the flower to help keep the filling inside. Proceed to cooking.
5. For raw preparations, simply cut crosswise into pieces or use whole petals; it's entirely up to you. I use the base of the blossom in raw preparations as well because I like its firmer texture and more vegetal-forward flavor. Also, waste not want not!

though many remove it. You can remove the prickly sepals that surround the base of the flower if you're eating the blossoms raw, but if you're cooking the blossoms, their prickly texture softens to something I can't detect. Again, let your palate be your guide. Personally, I like doing less work if I can, so I leave them on when I cook them.

COOKING TIPS: Squash blossoms are such a delicacy that I encourage you to keep any recipe you make with them fairly simple so that you may better taste their subtle flavor. Mexican cooks often prepare squash blossom quesadillas, which are incredible. They are served with a simple crema on top. This is no place for salsas or sriracha. Also popular in Mexico is a soup prepared with the blossoms and cooked zucchini. I prefer using a light vegetable stock when making this soup to let the flavors of the zucchini and blossoms shine. Using the blossoms both cooked and raw, and the zucchini both cooked and raw, is one of my favorite ways to highlight the diversity of flavors you can get from one plant (see the Squash Blossom and Squash Salad with Toasted Walnuts and Parmesan recipe on page 86 for an example of that).

SUBS: Besides using pumpkin blossoms for squash blossoms, there really isn't a great substitute. It's a special thing, entirely unique! Enjoy them when you can!

Squash Blossom and Squash Salad
with Toasted Walnuts and Parmesan

This is a simple recipe, all the better to highlight the freshness of the ingredients and the delicacy of squash blossoms. There's no room to hide, however, so make sure you are using high-quality ingredients. This recipe makes use of one key ingredient, squash, in four different ways: raw, salted, caramelized, and seared.

SERVES 4

10 ounces zucchini

½ teaspoon salt, plus more for sprinkling on zucchini

3 tablespoons olive oil

1 barely ripe peach, cut into 8 wedges

Black pepper, to taste

12 squash blossoms

½ cup walnuts, toasted

½ ounce Parmesan cheese, shaved

½ cup basil leaves

Drizzle of balsamic glaze (or thicken balsamic vinegar down to a glaze), about 2 tablespoons

Your best olive oil, for drizzling, about 2 tablespoons

Handful of nasturtium flowers and leaves or other edible flowers (optional)

Using a mandoline, carefully slice half of the zucchini into ⅛-inch lengthwise ribbons. Lightly sprinkle the slices with salt as you lay them down on a plate. Cut the other half of the zucchini into large cubes.

In a large skillet, heat 2 tablespoons of the olive oil over medium-high heat. When the pan is hot, sear the peaches and zucchini cubes, making sure that both sides of the peaches and at least two sides of the zucchini are nicely browned. Season with ½ teaspoon salt and a few grinds of black pepper. Remove to a plate. In the same pan, add the final tablespoon of olive oil and sear half of the squash blossoms. Flip them over when one side browns and remove them from the pan after the other side is browned.

To put it all together, twirl the zucchini ribbons onto the plate in a jaunty fashion. Place the peaches, zucchini cubes, and cooked squash blossoms in a similarly jaunty fashion. Sprinkle the platter with the walnuts, Parmesan cheese curls, and basil leaves (you can leave them whole or tear them into smaller pieces). Drizzle the balsamic glaze over the salad. You are aiming for a light anointment. Next, drizzle the olive oil over the salad. Now for the really fun part: if you found nasturtium leaves and flowers or you are using other edible flowers, sprinkle those all around and, finally, break off the petals of the remaining squash blossoms and garnish with those. Take a food photo, post on social media, and then sit down to eat. You better tag me.

Herby Ricotta-Stuffed Squash Blossoms
with Fig Vinegar and Grilled Bread

It wouldn't be a worthy exploration of the best ways to cook squash blossoms without including one that is stuffed with all the oozy, delicious things. It's a little fiddly getting the cheese into the blossom, but I've provided some tips on page 84. While you can certainly buy store-bought ricotta, homemade is sublime. The fried shallots are a lovely textural contrast to the yielding, melt-in-your-mouth blossoms. A quick grill or toast of your favorite rustic bread is a must if you want a comforting delivery vehicle for the vinegar-spiked, cheesy, blossomy goodness.

SERVES 4, MAKES 20 STUFFED
SQUASH BLOSSOMS

FOR THE RICOTTA MIXTURE
1 cup homemade Ricotta (see recipe on page 48, or use store-bought whole milk ricotta)
2 tablespoons shiso leaf (or mint), minced
1 tablespoon tarragon, minced
⅛ teaspoon freshly ground black pepper
½ teaspoon salt
Zest and juice from ½ lemon

FOR THE FRIED SHALLOTS
1 cup high-heat oil
1 medium shallot, cut into thin rings
Salt, as needed

FOR ASSEMBLY
20 squash blossoms
Olive oil, as needed
4 ounces zucchini, sliced thin
¼ teaspoon salt, plus more to taste
2 tablespoons fig vinegar (or balsamic vinegar)
2 tablespoons of your favorite olive oil
Flaky sea salt, as needed
¼ cup shiso or mint, chiffonaded
4 thick slices bread, grilled or toasted
½ lemon

TO MAKE THE RICOTTA MIXTURE
In a medium bowl, mix the ricotta with the shiso leaf, tarragon, black pepper, salt, and lemon zest and lemon juice.

TO FRY THE SHALLOTS
Heat the oil to 350°F in a small pot. Fry the shallots until they are crispy. Transfer them with a slotted spoon to a paper towel. Lightly sprinkle salt over the shallots as soon as they come out of the oil.

TO ASSEMBLE
Prepare the squash blossoms (see prep information on page 84). Pipe or spoon a scant amount of the ricotta mixture (no more than 2 teaspoons, depending on the size of the blossom) into each blossom and twist the end to seal.

Heat a large sauté pan over medium-high heat, add 1 tablespoon of olive oil and add the sliced zucchini and salt. Cook until browned, 4 to 5 minutes. Remove from the pan.

Add another tablespoon of olive oil to the pan and gently sear the stuffed squash blossoms on each side until they caramelize and the cheese just starts to ooze out, about 2 to 4 minutes total, depending on how big they are.

Lay the blossoms out on a serving tray. Garnish with the pieces of zucchini. Drizzle the fig vinegar, good olive oil, flaky sea salt, shiso leaves, and fried shallots over the squash blossoms. Serve with the grilled bread and a squeeze of lemon over the top.

Tempura Squash Blossoms *with Ponzu Sauce*

There was no way I could end this chapter without including a recipe for fried squash blossoms, one of the most satisfying ways to enjoy them. Tempura batter is famously light, which is helpful to preserve the elegance of the squash blossoms. I have included a recipe for homemade ponzu sauce, but feel free to use purchased ponzu if you are short on time. Or you can simply serve the fried blossoms with a simple squeeze of lemon at the table. You'll need to plan ahead if you use the homemade Shiitake Dashi (page 28), as it takes overnight to make the infusion.

SERVES 4

FOR THE PONZU SAUCE
3 scant tablespoons shiitake dashi (page 28) or instant dashi

3 scant tablespoons soy sauce (I prefer Yamasa brand)

2 tablespoons freshly squeezed citrus juice (a mixture of lemon/lime, grapefruit, or yuzu if you have access to it)

2 teaspoons toasted sesame oil

1½ teaspoons seasoned rice wine vinegar

1 teaspoon toasted white sesame seeds

1 teaspoon grated fresh ginger

FOR THE TEMPURA BATTER
½ cup unbleached all-purpose flour

½ cup white rice flour

1 teaspoon baking powder

½ teaspoon salt

⅛ teaspoon cayenne pepper

1 large egg yolk

1½ cups ice-cold water (chill the water with ice cubes before straining and measuring)

FOR FRYING
High-heat oil

12 large squash blossoms or 24 small ones

Salt, as needed

TO MAKE THE PONZU SAUCE
Mix all the ingredients together in a bowl. Set aside.

TO MAKE THE TEMPURA BATTER
Mix both flours, baking powder, salt, and cayenne together in a medium bowl using a whisk. Using chopsticks or a fork, add the dry ingredients to the egg yolk and cold water. The key here is to not mix very much at all. Lumps are good. Any energy in mixing the batter will develop gluten, making your tempura batter bready and heavy, the opposite of great tempura. The batter should be the consistency of thin pancake batter with lots of lumps. The ice-cold batter also slows gluten from developing, leading to a lighter and crispier squash blossom.

TO FRY THE BLOSSOMS
Heat 2 inches of oil to 360°F in a Dutch oven or heavy saucepot. Have a paper towel–lined plate or a brown paper bag at the ready to drain the tempura. Dip the squash blossoms into the batter and, using chopsticks, tongs,

or your fingers if you have cooked professionally (and no longer have nerve endings in your fingers), add to the oil. Fry in a few batches. Fry, flipping over once while cooking, until the blossoms are light brown, 3 to 4 minutes total cooking time. Use a skimmer to remove them and allow them to drain.

Lightly salt them. In between batches, use the skimmer to pull out any sediment floating in the oil. Make sure the temperature is between 350° and 370°F before you fry another batch.

Serve immediately with ponzu for dipping.

Tomatillos

AKA
PHYSALIS PHILADELPHICA,
PHYSALIS IXOCARPA, MEXICAN
HUSK TOMATO, JAMBERRY, HUSK
CHERRY, MEXICAN TOMATO

THE 411: Long before Europeans colonized Mexico and Central America, the Maya and Aztecs had domesticated tomatillos, favoring them over tomatoes. *Tomatillo* means "little tomato" in Spanish, and comes from the Nahuatl word *tomatl*. Tomatillos are in the nightshade family and closely resemble but are not the same as cape gooseberries and ground cherries (two fruits that should go into a *Misunderstood Fruits* book). The pulp and seeds inside the tomatillo are edible, but the husk (also known as the lantern), stems, and leaves of the tomatillo plant are toxic.

Tomatillos are bracingly tart, with a lemon-lime flavor plus a green note, a hint of cucumber, and maybe some green apple. It is especially acidic when raw and retains some of its acidity after being cooked. While they can be eaten raw in salads, salsas, or vinaigrettes, most recipes call for cooking them, either through boiling, grilling, or roasting. Roasting and grilling bring out some sweetness, which balances some of the acidity.

In the introduction to this book, I write about why I include tomatillos in this book (see page 10), but the TL;DR (too long; didn't read) shortened version on that is this: if you didn't grow up eating tomatillos, you might only know they're used in salsa, and you may not have any idea how to prepare them yourself. They are good in so much more than salsa! And yet, despite this, I'd be remiss not to include a tomatillo salsa recipe because they are so incredibly delicious. I even include a story about a tomatillo salsa that includes a bonus recipe (see box on page 100).

AKA: *Physalis philadelphica, Physalis ixocarpa,* Mexican husk tomato, jamberry, husk cherry, Mexican tomato.

NUTRITION FACTS: Tomatillos are rich in dietary fiber, antioxidants, potassium, manganese, and vitamin B_3.

SEASON: Tomatillos, similar to their nightshade relatives (tomatoes, eggplants, peppers, and so forth), are heat-seeking summer season vegetables.

PURCHASE, STORAGE, AND PREP TIPS: You'll find both green and purple varieties of tomatillo in the marketplace, though green is more widely available in the United States. As the fruit ripens, the husk turns from green to brown, and as the fruit grows it will start to peek through the drying, splitting husk. Green tomatillos start out green and ripen to yellow (which will be a bit sweeter). Purple tomatillos start out pale green and ripen to a deep violet. If you are looking for tomatillos to provide the acidity they are famous for, you can choose tomatillos that are still green. Check for ripeness by peeking under the husk. Make sure there are no soft spots or blemishes. Look for fruits that have filled their husks. If there is too much room left in the husk, the fruit is immature and will lack some depth of flavor. For the more common green tomatillo, I look for a bright green color inside and a split-open husk that is starting to dry and brown. When the tomatillo is quite ripe you will sometimes see a husk skeleton, a crime-scene outline of what was there before.

Store tomatillos in a produce bag, unhusked, in your crisper drawer. Use them within a few weeks. When you're ready to use them, simply remove the husks and . . . wait, what is that stuff all over my fingers? Tomatillos, like many plants, are engaging in some self-defense here. This protective sap contains withanolides, which is a substance that helps keep pests off the fruit because it tastes bad. Did I just call you a pest? Well, in a way, we are. This sap can cause some people to have skin reactions, so you might want to wear gloves if you know you are sensitive. I recommend you leave the protective sap on until you are ready to eat them. A simple light scrubbing under running water will wash off the stickiness. Isn't it nice that we are smarter than bugs? (Or are we?)

COOKING TIPS: Boiling instructions: Cook tomatillos in salted, simmering water until they turn drab green and soften, 8 to 10 minutes. Dry heat cooking: Char them until blackened in spots and cook only as long as you want—shorter times for firmer texture and more acidity, longer for a softer texture and more sweetness to balance the acidity. If you panfry tomatillos, as in the recipe for Fried Green Tomatillos with Chipotle Comeback Sauce on page 95, keep in mind that they soften a great deal when cooked, so a quick, hot fry is recommended lest they become mushy.

SUBS: Green tomatoes with lime juice, jalapeño chiles (seeded) with lime juice, green bell peppers with lime juice.

Tomatillo Math!

1 pound = 15 to 18 small tomatillos
1 pound = 8 to 10 medium tomatillos
1 pound = 11 ounces of husked, cooked
        tomatillos

Fried Green Tomatillos
with Chipotle Comeback Sauce

Tomatillos are so much like a green tomato crossed with a lime that I wondered what it would be like to cook them as you do in fried green tomatoes. Wonder no more! Unless you're a gardener, it's sometimes difficult to find green tomatoes but relatively easy to find tomatillos, so you can enjoy this dish whenever tomatillos are in the market. Make sure you cut a sliver off the round end pieces, exposing the inside of the tomatillo, as the slippery skin repels the batter. A quick, hot fry prevents the tomatillos from softening and getting mushy. You'll have extra comeback sauce to use as a dip, salad dressing, or a whole 'nother batch. The original "comeback sauce" comes from The Rotisserie, a Greek restaurant in Jackson, Mississippi, so named because, "You come back now, ya hear?"

SERVES 4

FOR THE COMEBACK SAUCE

1 cup Greek yogurt

¼ cup ketchup

2 tablespoons mayonnaise

2 teaspoons Dijon mustard

2 teaspoons green Tabasco, more if needed

¼ teaspoon chipotle chile powder, more if needed

¼ teaspoon salt

¼ teaspoon freshly ground black pepper

FOR THE TOMATILLOS

2 cups high-heat oil

1½ pounds tomatillos (pick the biggest ones you can find for this)

1 cup buttermilk (or whole milk)

1 teaspoon to 1 tablespoon Crystal or other hot sauce

½ cup panko (or gluten-free panko)

½ cup cornmeal

½ teaspoon salt

Flaky salt, as needed

TO MAKE THE COMEBACK SAUCE

In a medium bowl, combine all the ingredients together with a whisk. Taste and adjust the heat level by adding more chipotle chile powder or Tabasco. Chill until you are ready to eat.

TO MAKE THE TOMATILLOS

Preheat the oil to 375°F in a large cast-iron skillet or similar heavy-bottomed skillet while you prepare the tomatillos.

Slice the tomatillos into ½-inch rounds. In a medium bowl, mix the buttermilk and hot sauce. In a paper bag (or other bag) combine the panko with the cornmeal and salt.

Add the tomatillos to the buttermilk mixture and make sure they are well coated. Pull 2 or 3 slices out of the mixture, tap off excess, and place right into the paper bag. Shake the bag a few times and move the now battered

continues ➡

tomatillos onto a baking sheet (don't batter more than a few at a time for best coverage).

Once all the tomatillos are battered, you are ready to fry! Have a baking sheet ready with a cooling rack on top of it. Add 5 or 6 rounds at a time to the oil. As soon as they turn golden brown and feel crispy (lift the tomatillo out of the oil and lightly scrape the back of your fingernail along the surface to make sure it's not soft), about 1 to 2 minutes, flip and cook for just another 30 to 45 seconds and remove to the cooling rack. Immediately sprinkle some flaky salt on the fried tomatillos while the oil is still wet for best stickage. Make sure to skim any bits out of the oil with a fine mesh sieve tool between batches and recheck the temperature to make sure it's roughly around the 365° to 385°F range before frying another batch.

Enjoy right away served with the comeback sauce.

Charred Tomatillos *with Burrata, Peach,*
Basil, and Croutons

This recipe walks the line between raw and cooked tomatillos, charring them over high heat for just long enough to get some flavor on them while preserving their crisp texture. The tomatillos, along with the tomatoes, provide the tart acidity in this recipe, making a vinaigrette unnecessary. Simply drizzle your best olive oil over the top with some nice flaky salt and you have a new take on the traditional panzanella salad.

SERVES 6

FOR THE VEGETABLES

2 tablespoons olive oil

½ pound tomatillos, husked, rinsed, and medium diced

1 teaspoon salt, divided

1 tablespoon honey

2 slightly underripe peaches, cut into ¾-inch pieces

2 serrano chiles (1 seeded, if you want less heat)

FOR THE CROUTONS

4 cups rough-torn artisan bread (in bite-sized pieces)

3 tablespoons olive oil

½ teaspoon salt

FOR ASSEMBLY

6 ounces burrata

½ pint cherry tomatoes, cut in half

½ bunch basil, torn roughly

1 tablespoon of your best-quality olive oil, for finishing

Flaky sea salt

TO COOK THE VEGETABLES

In a large sauté pan over high heat, add 1 tablespoon of the oil and, after a moment, add the tomatillos and ½ teaspoon of the salt. Cook the tomatillos until they are charred in spots and darken in color but still retain texture, 5 to 6 minutes. Add the honey and cook for 30 more seconds. Remove the tomatillos to a plate. Add the other 1 tablespoon of oil to the pan, turn the heat down to medium-high and sear the peaches and the whole serrano chiles (no need to remove the stem), adding the remaining ½ teaspoon salt. The peach slices should caramelize a bit and the chiles should soften and blacken, about 4 to 5 minutes. Watch the peaches carefully, as they burn easily. When the peaches are caramelized on both sides, remove them to the plate with the tomatillos. The serranos may take a minute or two longer to char. When the chiles are cool, slice them into thin rounds (if you've seeded them, just slice the halves into half rounds).

continues ➤

TO MAKE THE CROUTONS

Preheat the oven to 400°F. Toss the bread with the olive oil and salt and bake until slightly crispy (leaving them a bit soft in the middle helps to absorb some of the juices of the salad), 10 to 15 minutes.

TO ASSEMBLE

On a wide platter, lay out the charred tomatillos, peaches, and slices of serrano chile. Cut the burrata into chunks or break it up with your fingers and scatter it around the salad along with the cherry tomatoes, torn bread croutons, and basil. Drizzle on the olive oil and add flaky salt, especially on the burrata.

Pinche Salsa!

Tears are streaming down our faces as the smoke chokes us, filling our eyes, our lungs, our dribbling noses. It's the price we pay for learning the secrets to our friend Rosa's salsa. We have a big fire going in the backyard, we're drinking beers, and she's telling us about her family making this salsa in Colima, Mexico. I'm trying to drink a beer and turn tomatoes while holding a red bandana over my face. It's a look. Rosa is helping and directing. She tastes the first batch out of the blender. "More jalapeños." Always more chiles. Why not, I think, I'm already dying. The tomatillos are boiling in a pot in the kitchen. We've dragged the blender out to the backyard and we're sterilizing 40 jars in a huge pot that could bathe a few babies. Rosa's wife, Radha, is going back to their house (just down the block) to pick more tomatoes. "You should put this in your book," says Rosa. I quickly imagine writing up a recipe that could feed a small country and smile while considering ingredient amounts by the handfuls and bagfuls. "You got it," I say, "probably in a sidebar, since I already wrote that most people already connect tomatillos to salsa." We clink beers and wipe our noses, coughing out smoke. What should we call it? "Pinche salsa!" she says.

Here's the "recipe": Smoke and char as many tomatoes as you and your neighbors can grow or you can drag back from a farmers' market. Don't use heirloom tomatoes—they are too watery; you want beefsteak tomatoes, although I bet Romas would work well, too. Add as many jalapeños and serrano chiles to the fire as you dare. Add more. Always more. Smoke (burn) those, too. Bring a big pot of tomatillos to a boil until they turn olive green, about 10 minutes (use about one-quarter the amount of the tomatoes—don't weigh, just eyeball this). Now here's the scientific part: throw everything into a blender in batches, puree, add handfuls of salt, and taste 4,000 times. At some point, fry up some tortilla chips, though you can buy them of course. Taste 4,000 more times. Drink more beer. Burn your hands pulling the jars out of the boiling water. Fill all the jars and process in a canning pot. Eat through your allotment of 15 jars within 2 weeks. Regret not making more. Feel free to make smaller batches, but why?

Chilaquiles *with Charred Tomatillo-Serrano Salsa*

Chilaquiles are commonly served with either red or green salsa; however, I prefer splitting the difference with chilaquiles divorciados, *where both red and green salsa are used. I'd like to think that to compromise with this much flavor makes for a good marriage, not a divorce. I love how the red salsa brings smoky, savory notes to the dish, while the acidic tomatillo salsa cuts through the richness of the fried chips, eggs, and avocado. Leave the seeds in the chiles if you know you love heat. Cilantro stems are delicious and can get pureed along with the leaves into the salsa for a flavorful waste-free sauce. Simply cut off the very bottom of the bunch and go from there. There is no need to make your own tortilla chips, but let me tell you how over the top this dish gets when you take the time to do it. It's not that hard, and the frying oil can simply be saved in your refrigerator for when you make this dish again.*

SERVES 4

FOR THE ANCHO-TOMATO SALSA

2 dried ancho chiles (use only 1 if you want a
    less spicy sauce), stems and seeds removed
2 tablespoons olive oil
1 small yellow onion, small diced
¼ teaspoon salt, plus more to taste
2 large red tomatoes, cored and quartered
½ teaspoon honey, plus more to taste
1 cup water

FOR THE TOMATILLO-SERRANO SALSA

1 tablespoon high-heat oil
1 pound tomatillos, husked and rinsed
1 serrano chile
2 garlic cloves, smashed
1 teaspoon salt, plus more to taste
1 teaspoon honey
1 small bunch cilantro (save some leaves
    for garnish)

FOR THE FRIED TORTILLA CHIPS

1 cup high-heat oil
20 corn tortillas, each tortilla cut into
    8 triangles
Salt

FOR THE TOPPINGS

2 ounces queso fresco or queso cotija
1 cup Mexican crema (or sour cream
    or yogurt)
1 avocado, pitted, peeled, and sliced right
    before serving
4 large eggs, fried over easy
Tomatillo-Serrano Salsa
¼ cup pumpkin seeds, toasted
Reserved charred and diced tomatillos
2 radishes, julienned (optional)
1 can refried beans, warmed (optional)
2 limes, cut into wedges (optional)

TO MAKE THE ANCHO-TOMATO SALSA

In a large cast-iron skillet or frying pan over medium-high heat, toast the ancho chiles by spreading them out and toasting them for a few minutes on each side (no oil needed). They will become aromatic and pliable. In a heatproof bowl or in a saucepot, pour boiling water over them to rehydrate for 10 minutes.

continues ➡

Heat the olive oil over medium-high heat in the same skillet you used for the ancho chiles. Add the onion and salt and sauté for 8 to 10 minutes. Add a tablespoon or two of the chile rehydration liquid from the saucepan if the onion starts to stick or gets too dried out. When the onions are soft and lightly browned, about 10 minutes, transfer them to a blender. Scoop out the anchos from the liquid and add them to the blender, along with the tomatoes and honey. You can discard the chile-soaking liquid or use it in place of the 1 cup of water if you're not worried about the added spiciness. Blend into a smooth puree and season to taste with salt and honey. (Go light on the salt if you will be using already-salted purchased tortilla chips in the dish.) Pour the chile sauce into the small saucepan along with 1 cup of water (or the chile-soaking liquid), bring to a boil, lower the heat to a simmer, and cook for 10 minutes. Keep warm and taste for seasoning.

TO MAKE THE TOMATILLO-SERRANO SALSA
Using that skillet one more time, heat 1 tablespoon of high-heat oil over medium-high heat. When the pan is hot, add the tomatillos and serrano and cook until they turn brown and lightly charred in places. You want the tomatillos to turn from bright green to drab green in most places and to soften up a bit. This should take 7 to 10 minutes of cooking time. Remove 2 tomatillos, let cool, and then chop into medium dice for garnish. Remove the seeds and membranes from the serrano for a less spicy sauce or leave them in and simply take off the stem. Place the serrano along with the tomatillos, garlic, salt, honey, and cilantro (stems and all) in a blender and puree until smooth. Season to taste with more salt if necessary.

TO MAKE THE FRIED TORTILLA CHIPS
Add the vegetable oil to the skillet and heat to 350°F. Set up a baking sheet with several layers of paper towels on it. Working in batches, slip as many tortilla triangles as will fit and not overlap into the skillet. Flip them over with tongs when they start to brown, about 2 to 3 minutes. Remove from the oil with a slotted spoon or grab a bunch with your tongs, letting as much oil as possible drain back into the skillet. Spread the chips out on the paper towels. Repeat until all the tortilla chips are fried. Sprinkle salt, to your liking, on the fried tortilla chips right away so the salt sticks to the oil clinging to the chips.

TO FINISH THE DISH
To prepare each plate, dunk one-quarter of the chips into the ancho-tomato salsa, turning them all around with your tongs. Knock off any extra sauce and place on the plate. Pour the tomatillo-serrano salsa all around the outside of the plate. Add on any or all of the toppings.

Fall

Beets

AKA

BETA VULGARIS, BEETROOT,
EUROPEAN SUGAR BEET, RED
GARDEN BEET, HARVARD BEET,
BLOOD TURNIP, CANDY CANE
BEETS

THE 411: If I had known as a child that the Latin for beets was *Beta vulgaris,* it wouldn't have surprised me a bit. In the 1980s when I was a kid, beets came from a can and I called them earthturds. They tasted like dirt to me, but worse. And I knew what I was talking about because I'd eaten my fair share of dirt, being a kid and all. An organic compound (geosmin) is responsible for the earthy flavor of beets. This same compound is found in spinach and mushrooms. Unsurprisingly, human beings are super sensitive to this compound, which explains why these ingredients can be divisive. To be perfectly honest, while I do eat beets from time to time, they are not my favorite vegetable, especially if they are prepared incorrectly. They have specific needs, and that's precisely why they are misunderstood. My chef friend Abby has mastered them, and her recipe in this chapter has made me a convert. The secret? Tons of acidity to balance the sweetness, something fatty to lightly blanket the earthiness. When you reach for beets, you should learn to reflexively reach for citrus, vinegar, nuts, cheeses, yogurt, or sour cream each and every time.

Humans have been eating beets for a very long time. They were originally domesticated in the Middle East; and the Greeks, Romans, and ancient Egyptians grew beets, primarily for their greens. If the ancients were watching us in our kitchens, they'd be horrified to see how many of us stare at the beet greens and go, hmmm, and then throw them away. Beets have been used as a food, as a dye for wine, and as a treatment

Beets That Won't Make You Call 911

If the "surprise" colorant effect of common red beets freaks you out, and every time you eat them you forget it's the beets that are the source of all that red (nope, you're not bleeding internally), you might want to explore the other colors.

- **Golden beets:** Milder than the red ones, both in earthiness and sweetness, golden beets bring some lovely sunshine into your kitchen at a time when the days get shorter. Plus, your countertop doesn't look like a murder scene after you cut them up.
- **Chioggia beets:** Not to be confused with Chioggia radicchio (Chioggia is a region of Italy where these cultivars originated), this type of beet is striped in vivid pink and white. They are the sweetest variety, and you can find them at farmers' markets.
- **White beets:** Less common and a bit harder to find, white beets are less sweet than other types. They look a bit like small white turnips.

(Bartolomeo Platina, a 15th-century Italian Renaissance gastronomist and humanist, used beets to nullify "garlic breath," which paints a lovely picture of someone stinking like garlic with bright red teeth saying "come here and kiss me"). They are especially revered in eastern Europe, the birthplace of Ukranian borscht, a dish that spread to other countries with countless variations.

Beets are in the same family as chard. Look closely at beet stems and leaves, and you'll notice how similar they are to chard. The stems and leaves can be cooked in exactly the same manner, so save them for chard recipes, such as those starting on page 126.

AKA: *Beta vulgaris,* beetroot, European sugar beet, red garden beet, Harvard beet, blood turnip. Chioggia beets are sometimes called candy cane beets.

NUTRITION FACTS: Beets have high amounts of fiber, folate, vitamin A, manganese, potassium, vitamin C, and other antioxidants.

SEASON: Fall is prime season for beets, but you can dig them up in late summer and also into winter.

PURCHASE, STORAGE, AND PREP TIPS: Look for smaller, early-season beets for the sweetest, least earthy flavor. Early season beets often have pristine tops, as well.

If you like eating beets raw, early fall is the time to make those recipes. As beets mature, they get bigger, more earthy, and better for cooking. In general, look for beets that are firm with no soft spots. The best way to get fresh beets is to buy them with fresh—not limp and sad—greens attached. Beets store well for a long time, up to a month, so if you buy them with the greens attached you know that they were recently harvested and full of vitality. To store beets, cut the greens from the roots and store separately. Don't wash either until you use them to avoid moisture-related mold issues. Wrap the greens in dry paper towels and put them in a produce bag. Store the beets in a produce bag. Store both in the crisper drawer. When you are ready to cook the beets and greens, wash them both thoroughly. Leave the skins on the beets if you are going to be roasting them, as it's quite easy to get the peel off after it's cooked. If you are eating the beets raw, I recommend peeling them unless you don't mind the texture of the peel. The peels are perfectly edible and nutritious, so do eat them if you're into it. Separate the stems from the leaves, as the stems take longer to cook than the leaves.

COOKING TIPS: There are several methods to cook beets. You can boil or pressure cook them, which is the fastest way to go (keep in mind, you lose nutrients unless you use the cooking liquid). You can coat them in some oil, wrap them in foil, and roast them in a hot oven—a temperature range of 375° to 425°F—and except for dealing with the hot ball of foil, it's an easy way to go. Some cooks put an inch or so of water in the bottom of a pan, add the whole beets to the pan with a splash of oil and some salt, and then cover and bake that way. No matter which way you go, make sure the beets are tender inside. If a knife can be inserted easily, they're done. Depending on the size of the beets, they will usually take 30 to 60 minutes to roast this way. Less time is needed at a higher heat, naturally. Let them cool a bit, don some gloves—unless you want to run around the house pretending you murdered someone with your bare hands (a good bit of fun)—and slide the peels off the beets. I like to do this over a bowl or garbage can, as red beet juice stains everything, especially wooden cutting boards.

SUBS: To be perfectly honest, there is no great substitute for beets. Luckily, beets are inexpensive and very easy to find in nearly every grocery store. If you want to make a recipe that contains beets and you simply don't like them, red cabbage will give you the color and some of the sweetness, but the texture and flavor will be different.

"Beetmus" with Pistachio Dukkah

Despite the fact that "beetmus" sounds like the name of a lesser holiday on Seinfeld, *it's more than just an awkward word baby; it's a portmanteau of beet and hummus. Adding a beet to hummus adds nutrition, a hint of sweetness and earthiness, and most notably, a stunning color makeover that screams for your attention. Feel free to double this recipe and use leftovers on sandwiches, tortilla roll-ups, and the like. For fish-eaters, it makes an unusual but delectable base for grilled or roasted salmon and black cod.*

SERVES 4 TO 6

1 medium red beet (4 to 6 ounces), scrubbed

3 tablespoons best quality olive oil, divided

One 15-ounce can garbanzo beans, drained and rinsed (or the equivalent in home-cooked beans)

Juice of 1 lemon (about ¼ cup), plus more to taste

3 tablespoons tahini (I recommend the brand Soom, which you can find online)

1 teaspoon salt, plus more to taste

Pistachio Dukkah (recipe follows)

Preheat the oven to 400°F.

Place the beet in a small ovenproof skillet, drizzle 1 tablespoon of the olive oil over the top of the beet, fill the bottom ½ inch of the skillet with water, and cover the skillet with foil. Roast for 30 to 45 minutes, until a knife slips easily in and out. When it cools enough to handle, put some gloves on or use a paper towel and slide off the peels. Cut the beet into chunks and add them to a blender or food processor along with all the other ingredients except the remaining 2 tablespoons olive oil and the dukkah (save the olive oil for drizzling on top). Puree to a very smooth consistency, adding a tiny bit of cold water if you want it thinned. Serve with some of the pistachio dukkah sprinkled on top and drizzle with the reserved olive oil.

PISTACHIO DUKKAH

Sumac can be found at fancier supermarkets, Middle Eastern markets, natural foods stores, or online. Dukkah can be stored at room temperature for a few weeks, or slightly longer in a cool and dark location. It's incredible sprinkled on dips, roasted vegetables, atop eggs, or as a garnish for soups—you'll have no problem using it up quickly.

MAKES 1 CUP

½ cup shelled pistachios

¼ cup pecans (or walnuts)

2 tablespoons sesame seeds

1 tablespoon whole coriander seeds

1 tablespoon whole cumin seeds

½ tablespoon fennel seeds

1 teaspoon sumac

1 teaspoon freshly ground black pepper

1 teaspoon salt, plus more to taste

Preheat the oven to 375°F.

Lay the pistachios and pecans out on a baking sheet. Toast in the oven for 8 to 10 minutes, until they are aromatic and lightly browned. Meanwhile, in a small skillet on the stove over medium-high heat, toast the sesame seeds until they are fragrant and light brown, about 1 to 2 minutes. Remove to a bowl. In the same skillet, toast the coriander, cumin, and fennel seeds for a few minutes until they are fragrant.

Grind the coriander, cumin, and fennel seeds (once toasted) to a powder in a spice grinder. Combine all the ingredients, including the reserved sesame seeds, together in a food processor or use a mortar and pestle to pulse or crush everything to a coarse texture. Taste for seasoning and then store in an airtight container.

Abby's Most Beautiful Beet Salad in the World

When I was asked to be the chef on a boat, I knew I didn't want to do the job alone because of all the work and no one to banter with, plus the long, lonely days at sea (that's a joke; we mostly do dinner cruises on a lake). So I recruited my good friend Abby to co-chef with me. We share a two-butt galley and have mostly merged into the same person after a few years of this. I wouldn't tell her this to her face because chefs and egos and all that, but her cooking inspires me and she pushes me to be better. She made this salad for our guests one night and I stood back and said, "Abz, that is the most beautiful beet salad in the world." And then, somehow, I convinced her to share the recipe and come with me to Vermont so she could style it for the camera (see the photo on page 114). You can toast the hazelnuts, roast the beets, and make the ricotta mixture and vinaigrette the day before you need them. You can have your own prep day, too, just like we do. Make this salad with a good buddy and bump butts in the kitchen—it's the only way to make beautiful food together.

SERVES 4

½ cup hazelnuts

¼ cup plus 2 tablespoons olive oil, divided, plus additional for hazelnuts

½ teaspoon salt, divided, plus more to taste

3 pounds baby beets, a mix of red, gold, and Chioggia if you can find them

Freshly ground black pepper, to taste

¼ cup red wine vinegar

1 red onion, sliced into paper-thin ¼-inch half-moons

2 oranges, cara cara or blood oranges for extra color

1 cup homemade Ricotta (recipe on page 48, or use store-bought whole milk ricotta)

½ teaspoon crushed pink peppercorn

2 tablespoons balsamic vinegar

1 teaspoon honey

1 teaspoon Dijon mustard

Microgreens of your choice or a handful of baby arugula, for garnish

Preheat the oven to 400°F.

Toast the hazelnuts on a baking sheet for 8 to 10 minutes, until they are lightly browned and aromatic. Keep a close eye on them. Once they've cooled off a bit, you can roll them in a towel to remove some of the skins (which can be bitter to some). You can crush the hazelnuts with a small bowl or jar rather than trying to chop them with a knife, which is a bit like chasing a cherry tomato around a plate with a fork. Toss the crushed hazelnuts with just enough of the olive oil to make them shiny and a pinch of salt. This pumps up the flavor of the hazelnuts and makes them look pretty on top of the salad.

Trim the stems and roots from the beets and wash the beets well. In a baking dish, toss the beets with 2 tablespoons of the olive

continues ➤

oil, ¼ teaspoon of salt, and some freshly ground pepper. Add enough water to cover the bottom of the dish with about ¼ inch of water. Cover the baking dish with foil and pop it in the oven. Bake until the beets are just tender, about 45 minutes. The beets are ready when you can easily pierce them with a knife.

Now that the beets are busy doing their thing, pour yourself a beverage and make some pickled red onions. In a small bowl, pour the red wine vinegar over the onions. Add ⅛ teaspoon of salt. Mix well. Let the onions pickle at room temperature for at least 30 minutes (1 hour is better), stirring occasionally.

Next, zest the oranges and set the zest aside for later. Slice both ends off the oranges and set them upright on a cutting board so they don't roll around. Start at the top and slice the remaining peel and pith from the juicy insides, following the curve of the orange. You can squeeze any remaining juice from the peels into a small dish for the vinaigrette. Slice the oranges into thin rounds and set them aside until you're ready to build the salad.

Mix the ricotta with half of the orange zest, the pink peppercorn, and ⅛ teaspoon of salt. Taste it to make sure it's delicious.

To make the salad dressing, whisk the balsamic vinegar, honey, Dijon, and the other half of the orange zest together with any orange juice you saved. While whisking, slowly drizzle in about ¼ cup of olive oil. Add a pinch of salt and a few cracks of freshly ground black pepper. Taste again!

By now the beets should be finished cooking. Remove the pan from the oven and uncover the beets. Allow them to cool just enough to handle. The skins should just rub off with gloved hands or a towel that you don't mind turning beet colors. Depending on the size of the beets, cut them in halves or smaller wedges. Toss the pieces with enough vinaigrette to make them shiny and tasty.

To assemble the salad, spread the pink peppercorn ricotta in a shallow serving bowl. Arrange the dressed beet pieces and orange rounds over the ricotta. Sprinkle with pickled red onion and greens of choice, and finish with the toasted and seasoned hazelnuts. If there is any of the vinaigrette left, drizzle it over the top of everything. Take a moment to admire *your* most beautiful beet salad in the world and dig in!

Not Your Ordinary Borscht

It has been said that there are as many variations of borscht as there are cooks in Ukraine. So the title of this recipe is tongue-in-cheek, as there is hardly an "ordinary" borscht. Each cook would say theirs is extraordinary. It's worth seeking out beets with their greens attached so you can see just how versatile this ingredient is: the root colors the soup; the stems, cut into short lengths, stew away with the other ingredients; and the beet greens cook for just a short time at the very end. One bunch of beets, all parts eaten. No wonder beets have been eaten for centuries, especially in cold climates with very short growing seasons.

SERVES 4

1 large beet, about 6 ounces (with stems and greens, if possible)

2 cups water

2 teaspoons salt, divided

1 bay leaf

2 tablespoons olive oil

1 large onion, sliced thin

1 pinch crushed red pepper flakes

2 garlic cloves, minced

6 to 8 ounces cabbage, chopped into bite-sized pieces or strips

1 pound squash (can use kabocha, butternut, or other firm, sweet squash of your choice), medium diced

½ cup dry white vermouth

2 cups vegetable stock or water

One 14-ounce can whole tomatoes, medium diced in the can, plus juice (I like Muir Glen brand)

1 carrot, julienned into fine threads

Salt, to taste

Freshly ground black pepper, to taste

1 bunch chives, thinly sliced, for garnish

¼ cup dill, roughly chopped, for garnish

1 cup sour cream, as needed, for garnish

Rinse the beet, peel it, and cut it into large chunks. Bring the water to a boil in a small saucepan. Add 1 teaspoon of the salt, beet pieces, and bay leaf. Simmer until the beets are tender, about 20 minutes. Remove the bay leaf. Puree the beets with the cooking liquid in a blender until smooth. Set aside.

In a large soup pot, heat the oil over medium-high heat. Add the onions, red pepper flakes, and 1 teaspoon salt and cook, stirring frequently, until the onions soften and just begin to brown, about 10 minutes. Add the garlic, cabbage, and squash and stir for a minute. Turn the heat to high and deglaze the bottom of the pot with the vermouth. Cook for 1 to 2 minutes more and then add the stock, tomatoes and juice, beet stems (chopped into ½-inch pieces), and reserved beet puree. Cook for about 20 minutes, or until the squash is nice and tender.

Add the carrots and chopped beet greens if you have them. Cook for 10 more minutes. Season to taste with salt and pepper. Garnish with chives, dill, and sour cream.

Brussels Sprouts

AKA
BRASSICA OLERACEA
VAR. GEMMIFERA,
MINI CABBAGES

THE 411: A nutrient-dense powerhouse in a tiny package, Brussels sprouts are in the *Brassica* genus, along with broccoli, cabbage, kale, collards, and kohlrabi. First cultivated near the Belgian city of Brussels in the 13th century, English speakers refer to them as "Brussels" sprouts, which is why Brussel sprouts without the "s" would be incorrect. In that classic game of "Which came first, the city or the vegetable?" it should come as no surprise that the city came first. Natives of Brussels simply call them sprouts (*spruiten* in Dutch); it's also why the French don't call their fries "French" fries but simply *frites*. Speaking of the French, in the 18th century, French settlers brought Brussels sprouts to Louisiana. In the United States today, California is the biggest producer, followed by Washington and New York states.

Cliché as it may be, many people still turn their noses up at the humble micro cabbage. The famed bitterness is more apparent if you personally carry the bitter taste receptor gene known as TAS2R38. This helps explain why some people refer to Brussels sprouts as the "cilantro" of the vegetable world. But as author J. Kenji López-Alt writes, Brussels sprouts "don't *need* to be the sulfurous, mushy, repulsive cabbages that you might have grown up eating." In fact, in the last 30 years or so, the "problematic" bitterness to some has been reduced by the breeding of sprouts with less of the glucosinolates (bitter compounds). Interestingly, these same compounds help protect Brussels sprouts from pests. What is more pleasant for humans is also more pleasant for pests, which is why nothing in life is easy.

AKA: *Brassica oleracea* var. *gemmifera* (*gemmiferous* means bud-producing), mini cabbages, "little green balls of death."

NUTRITION FACTS: High in antioxidant-rich vitamin C and vitamin K, with more moderate amounts of B vitamins (folate, vitamin B_6), Brussels sprouts are high in fiber and, along with others in the *Brassica* genus, may help reduce tumor growth.

SEASON: Fall through winter.

PURCHASE, STORAGE, AND PREP TIPS: If you live in the countries or US states where Brussels sprouts are widely cultivated, or you are a home gardener, you may be able to buy or harvest them still on the stalk. I did this not too long ago after seeing them at a local market in Washington State. I felt like an ambassador for this misunderstood vegetable as I hoisted my scepter of mini cabbage buds aloft, leading a parade of one.

Look for tight, vibrant green sprouts with

compact leaves, with little to no blemishes. Avoid any that are yellowing or browning. Choose ones around 1 to 1½ inches in diameter. The sprouts should be hard to the touch when you squeeze them. Considered sweetest after a frost, wait for the first cold snap of the season to buy or harvest. Once at home, they can last as long as a month if kept in near-freezing conditions. If you have a really cold cellar, they can hang out there while you figure out all that you want to use them for. They will last a few weeks in the fridge in a produce bag in your crisper drawer.

COOKING TIPS: Supremely misunderstood, especially when boiled to within an inch of their lives, Brussels sprouts shine when prepared correctly. The secret is high heat, which adds sweetness and depth of flavor thanks to browning. (Browning is an incredibly complex chemical process; it's known as the Maillard reaction.) High heat also adds crispness, which is a welcome contrast to the tender, nearly creamy centers. You'll find many recipes call for keeping them whole and scoring an X in the bottom, but I find that to be a tedious and unnecessary step. I prefer cutting them in half, right through the stem. This exposes more of the interior of the sprout to the high heat for browning and shortens the cooking time. The center of the sprout contains the bulk of the bitter compounds, so exposing that part to the sweetening effects of high heat will help to offset some bitterness. While I don't have a recipe for deep-frying sprouts in this book, if you're comfortable with hot oil, deep-fried Brussels sprouts are delightful.

SUBS: Broccoli, cabbage, and kohlrabi all make excellent substitutes for Brussels sprouts.

Crunchy Brussels Sprout Leaves *with Pickled Green Apple and Toasted Pecans*

I like to serve this dish to folks who don't like Brussels sprouts but do like cabbage as an attempt to convince them of the glory of sprouts. The key to this recipe is separating the leaves so they have space to stretch out, crisp up, and brown. The crispiness is a game changer. While it's a little fussy to pull the leaves off the sprouts, doing so creates a lot of surface area that becomes extra crispy in the hot oven. Leftover pickling liquid, which is lightly flavored with Granny Smith apple, can be saved in the fridge and used for salad dressings.

SERVES 4

1 pound Brussels sprouts, leaves removed

FOR THE GRANNY SMITH VINAIGRETTE
½ Granny Smith apple, unpeeled, large diced
½ cup olive oil
¼ cup apple cider vinegar
1 teaspoon salt
Freshly ground black pepper, to taste

FOR THE PICKLED APPLE
½ Granny Smith apple, small diced
½ cup seasoned rice vinegar

FOR THE GARNISHES
½ cup pecans, toasted, roughly chopped
2 tablespoons soft herbs such as dill, fennel, mint
2 ounces goat cheese, crumbled over the top

Preheat the oven to 450°F. Line a baking sheet with parchment paper.

Cut the ends off the sprouts and pull off loose leaves. Cut a bit more off the stem and continue pulling loose leaves. Save the core for roasting or slice for use in a salad.

TO MAKE THE VINAIGRETTE AND COOK THE SPROUTS
Puree the ingredients in a blender or with an immersion blender. In a medium bowl, take half of the vinaigrette and toss with the sprout leaves. Lay them out on the parchment paper and roast for 15 to 20 minutes. Watch them carefully—you want them crispy but not incinerated.

TO MAKE THE PICKLED APPLE
Pickle the other half of the apple by putting it in a jar and covering with the rice vinegar. Put the lid on the jar, shake it up, and let it sit until you need it. Drain the apple pieces when you're ready to serve them, saving the pickling liquid for another use.

TO ASSEMBLE
Pour the remaining vinaigrette onto a platter. Pile the roasted sprout leaves in the middle of the dressing. Garnish with the pecans, soft herbs, goat cheese, and pickled apples.

Roasted Brussels Sprouts *with Chestnuts, Pomegranate, and Honey*

This easy one-pan dish makes use of some key pantry ingredients that zhuzh up things with no effort: pomegranate molasses and already roasted and peeled chestnuts (both found in well-stocked grocery stores or online). The optional pomegranate seed garnish makes this dish feel just right for the holidays, and adds color and a satisfying pop of acidity. For a regular night, consider adding some seedy bread, roasted sweet potatoes, and a light salad for a complete meal. If you're a meat eater, add bacon or pieces of pancetta to the pan when you roast the sprouts.

SERVES 4

2 pounds Brussels sprouts

3 tablespoons plus ½ teaspoon olive oil, divided

½ teaspoon salt, plus a small pinch for the apple slices

1 apple

1 tablespoon pomegranate molasses

1 tablespoon balsamic vinegar

1 teaspoon honey

¼ teaspoon cayenne or crushed red pepper flakes (optional)

½ pound roasted chestnuts (cooked, peeled, and ready to eat), roughly chopped

1 pomegranate, seeded, for garnish (optional)

1 small branch rosemary, leaves snipped into tiny sprigs, for garnish (optional)

Preheat the oven to 450°F. Line a baking sheet with parchment paper.

Clean the sprouts and cut in half through the stem. On the baking sheet, toss the halved sprouts with 2 tablespoons of the olive oil and ½ teaspoon of the salt. Lay the sprouts out on the parchment paper, cut side down. Roast for about 30 minutes, or until caramelized on both sides and a knife slips easily in and out.

While the sprouts are roasting, slice the apple (peel on) into ¼-inch slices, heat up ½ teaspoon of olive oil in a large skillet over medium-high heat and, after a minute, add the apple slices with a small pinch of salt. Cook until browned on both sides, about 1 minute per side. In a small bowl, mix the remaining 1 tablespoon olive oil with the pomegranate molasses, balsamic vinegar, honey, cayenne, and chestnuts.

When the sprouts are done, pull them out of the oven and drizzle the pomegranate molasses–chestnut mixture over the top. Mix up everything well. Transfer to a serving bowl and garnish with the caramelized apples and optional pomegranate seeds and rosemary sprigs.

Maple-Glazed Brussels Sprouts *with Preserved Lemon, Hazelnuts, and Shiitake Bacon*

Did you know that mushrooms share more DNA with humans than humans do with plants? I think that's why they taste so "meaty." (How many vegan readers just threw this book at the wall because I wrote that? I'm sorry, but it's SCIENCE.) If you like mushrooms, you'll love shiitake bacon. Feel free to double the batch so you'll have some leftovers. It would be great thrown in the Char-Fried Cabbage with Ginger and Sesame (page 186) or the Rice Cake Soup with Turnips, Mushrooms, and Spicy Chile Oil (page 252). The sweetness from the maple syrup, combined with the acidity and funk of preserved lemons, complements the sprouts beautifully.

SERVES 6 TO 8

FOR THE SHIITAKE BACON
1 ounce dried shiitake mushrooms
2 teaspoons gluten-free tamari or soy sauce
1 teaspoon olive oil
Pinch of smoked salt or regular salt, to taste

FOR THE BRUSSELS SPROUTS
2 pounds Brussels sprouts, trimmed and halved
¼ cup olive oil
1 tablespoon maple syrup
½ teaspoon salt

FOR THE GARNISHES
½ cup hazelnuts, toasted, roughly chopped
½ preserved lemon, peel only, julienned
1 lemon, cut in half
A few tablespoons of your favorite olive oil
Pinch of flaky sea salt, to taste

Preheat the oven to 425°F. Line a baking sheet with parchment paper.

TO MAKE THE SHIITAKE BACON
Rehydrate the shiitake mushrooms in 1 cup of boiling water and let stand for 30 minutes. Once rehydrated, de-stem the mushrooms (save the stems for stock) and cut the mushroom caps into ¼-inch slices. Toss the mushrooms in the tamari, olive oil, and smoked salt. Set aside.

TO MAKE THE BRUSSELS SPROUTS
Toss the Brussels sprouts with the olive oil, maple syrup, and salt. Lay them cut side down on the baking sheet and roast for 20 minutes. Sprinkle the shiitake mushrooms over the top and cook for 10 to 15 minutes longer, until the shiitakes are browned and the sprouts are caramelized and tender.

TO ASSEMBLE
Place the sprouts and shiitakes on a serving platter and garnish with hazelnuts and preserved lemon. Squeeze ½ lemon over the top, drizzle with olive oil, sprinkle with flaky sea salt, and taste. Add more lemon juice if you'd like.

Chard

AKA
BETA VULGARIS, SWISS
CHARD, SPINACH BEET, SILVER
BEET, PERPETUAL SPINACH,
BEET SPINACH, SEAKALE
BEET, LEAF BEET, STEM
CHARD, ROMAN KALE

THE 411: Chard is a coastal plant native to Sicily. Often referred to as "Swiss" chard, probably because a Swiss botanist was the first to give the plant a scientific name, chard is grown and used all over the world (including in Switzerland). Of all the healthy greens to eat (kale, spinach, beet greens, and the like), chard is the most mild in flavor. Any bitterness that is detected in the leaves and stems of raw chard is mitigated when cooked.

There are numerous varieties of chard, but the ones you are most likely to see in the market are red chard, green chard, Orange Fantasia, and Barese (green leaves, white stems). Rainbow chard is often thought to be a variant of chard, but it is actually different-colored varieties bundled and sold together, much like a bouquet of flowers. You can buy rainbow chard seeds, but this is actually a mix of seeds from the different colors.

AKA: *Beta vulgaris,* Swiss chard, spinach beet, silver beet, perpetual spinach, beet spinach, seakale beet, leaf beet, stem chard, Roman kale.

NUTRITION FACTS: Chard is a super nutritious leafy green vegetable, with high amounts of vitamin A, K, and C, and the minerals magnesium, manganese, iron, and potassium. It is healthiest in the raw state but still nutritious when cooked.

SEASON: Fall is the main season for chard, but it also has a spring season. Though it grows quickly in cool temperatures (it can be harvested into the winter), it's tough enough to withstand hot temperatures. It makes a lovely, sturdy ornamental and edible plant during the summer.

PURCHASE, STORAGE, AND PREP TIPS: When purchasing chard, look for brightly colored, firm leaves that show no signs of wilting. There should be little bend to the stems. It should smell good! Look at the leaves and make sure there are few if any holes where pests may have had a snack. Make sure there is no discoloration or soft spots on the leaves or stem. To store chard, leave it unwashed to avoid moisture-related mold issues, and loosely wrap it in a paper towel and store in a produce bag in the crisper drawer. If the chard shows any signs of drying out, simply dampen the paper towel and rewrap. Chard will last for three to five days in the fridge. To prep, simply trim off the bottom of the stems and separate the stems from the leaves by using your knife to cut a "V" along the thicker, celery-like stem, separating the leaf on either side from the stem. Stems can be cut into two- to three-inch pieces and be sautéed, roasted, grilled, and so forth. Leaves can be rolled up and sliced thin or into bite-sized pieces, depending on what you are using it for.

COOKING TIPS: The most important tip for cooking chard is to separate the stems from the leaves, as they cook at different rates. Slice the stems crosswise and get them cooking at least 5 to 10 minutes before the greens to give them a head start.

SUBS: Swiss chard is basically a beet that was bred for its leaves and stems versus a large bulbous root. Beet greens are thicker and slightly more bitter than chard, but you can think of them as very close cousins. Spinach is in the same family as chard, and wherever you might use chard, you can sub with spinach. Kale would also make a great sub.

Charred Chard *with Spicy Chile Oil*

My friend Ashlyn and I were discussing chard recipes and got to talking about perhaps grilling it, and being that she's a pun lover, it quickly got into groan territory as she suggested we char the chard. I must admit, there is something super satisfying about saying it. How about charred chard over charcoal? Ashlyn was also voted most likely to say things like, "It's dill-licious" when I add dill to things. Serve this dish over rice cooked with coconut milk and top with a fried egg, or eat the charred chard on its own as an appetizer, perhaps alongside the Quick Pickled Daikon Radishes with Turmeric and Lime (page 147).

SERVES 4

2 bunches rainbow chard or any color
of chard
1 tablespoon Spicy Chile Oil (page 188) or
purchased chile oil
1 tablespoon peanut or vegetable oil
1 ounce ginger, grated
½ teaspoon salt
1 teaspoon sugar
1 teaspoon gluten-free tamari (or soy sauce)
1 teaspoon seasoned rice vinegar
Pickled chard stems (recipe follows;
optional)

Preheat a grill over high heat.

Prep the chard by washing, drying, and cutting the leaves from the stems as directed on page 127. In a large bowl, mix together the chile oil, peanut oil, ginger, salt, sugar, tamari, and rice vinegar. Add the chard leaves to the bowl with the marinade and toss the leaves through it well.

Grill the chard leaves until crispy and charred. Remove from the heat and slice into bite-sized pieces and serve with the pickled chard stems.

PICKLED CHARD STEMS

YIELDS 1½ TO 2 CUPS

Stems from 1 bunch rainbow chard or any
color of chard
1 cup seasoned rice vinegar

If the stems are quite wide (wider than an inch), split the stems by cutting them down the length. Cut the stems crosswise into ¼-inch pieces. Place the cut stems in a mason jar or other narrow container. In a small pot, bring 1 cup of seasoned rice vinegar to a boil. Remove from the heat and pour over the stems. If it doesn't quite cover the stems, add hot water until they are submerged under the liquid. Let the stems pickle in the vinegar for at least 30 minutes. Store in the refrigerator and use within a week or two.

Orecchiette *with Chard, Golden Raisins, Pine Nuts, Capers, and Chile*

This dish is on regular rotation in my house, especially on nights when we don't think we have much on hand to prepare and eat. It relies heavily on pantry staples, with the chard being the only fresh ingredient needed. Feel free to substitute the chard with cooked nettles, beet greens, mustard greens, turnip or kohlrabi greens, or a mixture of any and all.

SERVES 4

- 2 tablespoons plus ½ teaspoon salt, divided, plus more to taste
- ¼ cup white wine vinegar
- ⅓ cup golden raisins
- 2 bunches rainbow chard
- ¼ cup olive oil
- 1 onion, small diced
- ½ teaspoon crushed red pepper flakes
- 1 cup seasoned rice vinegar (for pickling the chard stems, recipe on page 129)
- ¼ cup dry white vermouth (or white wine)
- 1 tablespoon capers, drained
- ¼ cup pine nuts, toasted
- 1 pound dried orecchiette
- 3 ounces Parmesan cheese, grated (about 1 cup)

Bring water to a boil in a large soup pot. Add 2 tablespoons of the salt. In a small narrow jar, add the white wine vinegar to the raisins and stir. Set aside and set a timer for 15 minutes.

Remove the chard leaves from the stems as directed on page 127. Chop one-half of the stems into very fine slices (for pickling); the other one-half of the stems can be cut into ½-inch slices. Chop the leaves into bite-sized pieces. Drain the vinegar from the raisins and reserve the vinegar for salad dressings or other uses.

Meanwhile, in a large sauté pan over medium heat, add the olive oil. After a minute, add the onion along with ½ teaspoon salt. Cook the onion until it's tender, about 10 minutes. Add the ½-inch sliced chard stems and the red pepper flakes and cook for 2 to 3 minutes (reserve the other half of the stems for pickling—recipe on page 129). Add the chard leaves and sauté for a minute. Add the vermouth and deglaze the pan by scraping any brown bits off the bottom of the pan and incorporating them back into the onions. Add the reserved raisins, capers, and pine nuts and turn the heat to low.

Meanwhile, cook the orecchiette until it's al dente. Strain through a colander (saving ½ cup of the cooking liquid) and add the pasta to the sauté pan, along with the reserved cooking liquid. Turn the heat to medium and cook for another minute or two, stirring to incorporate the sauce into the pasta. Add half of the cheese, mix, and season to taste. Serve the pasta garnished with the rest of the cheese. Sprinkle the pickled chard stems over the top.

Rainbow Chard Shakshuka
with Pickled Chard Stems

Shakshuka is a dish of Maghrebi origin (Northwest Africa) that traditionally features eggs poached in tomatoes and spices. This green version omits the tomatoes in favor of a bounty of leafy greens and herbs. While chard is featured in this recipe, any of the edible greens (mustard, turnip, nettles, beet, kohlrabi, and so forth) can be used in this dish. In fact, save up your greens and make this dish to use them all up. It's a nutritious, incredibly flavorful dish that can be made at any time of the year.

SERVES 4

1 bunch rainbow chard

½ cup olive oil, divided

½ onion, small diced

1 jalapeño, small diced (seeded for less heat)

1 teaspoon salt, plus more to season eggs

1 bunch scallions, white and light green parts, sliced

1 bunch parsley

1 bunch cilantro

½ cup water, more if needed

¼ cup lime juice (from about 2 limes), plus 1 more lime for garnish

4 eggs

Freshly ground black pepper

3½ ounces sheep feta

1 cup basil leaves (from 1 small bunch)

1 cup fresh dill fronds (from 1 small bunch)

Harissa or your favorite hot sauce (optional)

4 pitas, toasted, grilled, or heated in a pan or in the oven

½ cup Pistachio Dukkah (page 112), for garnish (optional)

Separate the chard stems from the leaves. Pickle the stems according to the recipe on page 129.

Heat a large cast-iron skillet over medium-high heat. Add ¼ cup of the olive oil and cook the onion and jalapeño with 1 teaspoon salt until the onions soften up, about 10 minutes. Chop the chard leaves into bite-sized pieces and add in batches until they wilt down, about 2 to 3 minutes. Add the scallions and stir. Chop the parsley and cilantro, stems and all, into bite-sized pieces. Add to the pan and stir. Add ½ cup water and bring to a very gentle simmer. Lower the heat and cover, and let the greens stew for 15 minutes. Check on them occasionally and add a bit of water if it appears dry.

Add the lime juice and stir in. Make 4 divots in the greens for the eggs to sit in. Crack each egg and gently place in the divots. Season the eggs with a pinch of salt and freshly ground black pepper. Crumble the feta all around the eggs, leaving the tops of the eggs visible. Cover the pan and cook on medium-low heat. Check on the eggs every 2 minutes

until the eggs are cooked to your liking. I recommend cooking the eggs so the white is cooked through and the yolks are still runny.

Finish the dish by garnishing with the basil and dill, leaving some in a bowl on the side if people want extra. Have the harissa at the table as well as the pita. Serve with lime wedges and drizzle the remaining ¼ cup of your favorite olive oil over the top. If you made the dukkah, sprinkle some of that on top as well. Finally, sprinkle some of the pickled chard stems over the dish.

Celery Root

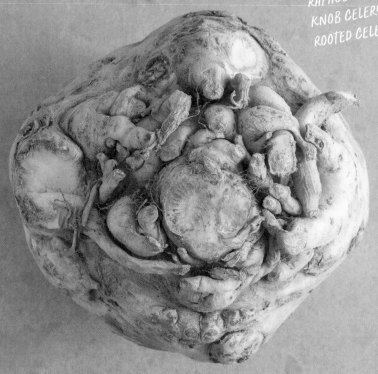

AKA
APIUM GRAVEOLENS VAR.
RAPACEUM, CELERIAC,
KNOB CELERY, TURNIP-
ROOTED CELERY

THE 411: In the Introduction of this book, I described how the checker at my local supermarket remarked that the celery root I had placed on the belt was "hideous." Were it not for that comment, this book might not be in your hands. Poor celery root. So misunderstood, so maligned by the ones who have not been let in on the secret that it's one of the best vegetables you might not know about. So, let's get to know this hideous thing.

Celery root, or celeriac as it's also commonly known, originated in the Mediterranean and was found growing wild by Swiss and Italian botanists. It's been cultivated since the 17th century and was brought to the United States in the 19th century. Today, it is widely grown around the world, from North Africa to Southwest Asia and North America. The main producers are in the Netherlands and central and eastern Europe.

A member of the carrot family, celery root is often thought to be the root of the common celery. The truth is that celery root has been selected for its bulb, while celery is grown for its crispy stems. They are related but not the same. While the flavors are similar, celery root is much denser, nearly potato-like, with a hint of the brightness that celery has but with a lovely nuttiness that is entirely its own.

AKA: *Apium graveolens* var. *rapaceum*, celeriac, knob celery, turnip-rooted celery.

NUTRITION FACTS: Extremely high in vitamin K, and high in fiber, phosphorus, and vitamins B_6 and C.

SEASON: Fall, extending into winter.

PURCHASE, STORAGE, AND PREP TIPS: Look for smooth celery roots (to help you peel it more easily) that have healthy-looking greens, if they are attached. Choose ones that feel heavy for their size, but not the largest ones unless they look impeccable (as they might have the hollow core that comes with age and advanced growth).

Celery root has a very long shelf life if it is kept between 32° and 41°F. In perfectly ideal conditions, it can stay fresh for months. Store in a closed container in your refrigerator for longer storage or in a bag in your crisper drawer for shorter-term storage. For longer-term storage you'll want to make sure no finer stems surrounding the base are left on, as they encourage rotting. When past its prime, a celery root will have a hollow center.

You will need to peel celery root, as the skin is thick and inedible. Use a knife to cut the top off, and cut the bottom off where the twisted roots meet the bulb. Lay it flat on a cutting board and use a knife to carefully cut off the peel. Make a cut that looks like a backward "C" as you work around the outside of the vegetable. Some people use a vegetable peeler, but I much prefer a chef's knife for its efficiency, toughness, and speed getting through the thicker skin. Make sure you have revealed the pure white interior and trimmed off any remaining peel. Proceed to cut into the size and shape required by the recipe, and store the cut root in acidulated water (squeeze a lemon into a bowl of cold water), as the root discolors fairly quickly. I don't bother doing this if I'm high-heat roasting celery root because it's going to get caramelized anyway.

COOKING TIPS: If you treat celery root as you would a potato, you already know how to cook it (boiled and mashed; roasted as fries; hash browns; and the like). For a simple fall lunch or dinner, cut celery root into thick "steaks," roast until tender and browned, and top with a lightly dressed herb salad with pumpkin seeds. And here's something superior about celery root as compared to the common potato: because potatoes are full of starch, when they get overworked in a food processor or mixer, that starch turns to glue. This won't happen with celery root, so no ricer, food mill, or masher is necessary: just pop the cooked root in a blender or food processor for making soups and mashers.

SUBS: Celery plus potato would get you the flavor plus the texture of celery root. Rutabaga or turnip could stand in. And for a similar texture but a much sweeter profile, try butternut squash.

Creamy Mashed Celery Root *with Horseradish and Rosemary Brown Butter*

Mashed potatoes are so 2003. Why 2003? No idea; I sort of randomly picked a year. But seriously, while I have nothing against mashed potatoes (and to be fair, they're pretty amazing), mashed celery root (and ooh ooh, one-half potato and one-half celery root) is also pretty amazing. It's mild, with just a hint of "Wait, what is this?" It's a conversation starter at the table and can give you and weird Uncle Sid something to talk about. Infusing rosemary (or sage or thyme—all are complementary to the flavor of celery root) into nutty browned butter, and then swirling that into the mix, turns what could be a humble root mash into a thing of noble splendor. This dish can be made a few days in advance and rewarmed with a splash of water or cream to loosen the mash.

SERVES 4

2 pounds celery root
1 medium shallot
1 tablespoon salt, plus more to taste
2 tablespoons unsalted butter
2 teaspoons fresh rosemary, minced
½ cup cream
1 tablespoon freshly grated horseradish or bottled horseradish cream
Reserved cooking liquid (from boiled celery root)
1 to 2 teaspoons lemon juice, to taste

Cut the peel off the celery root as instructed on page 135. Chop the celery root into large chunks. Slice the shallot into ¼-inch rounds. Place the celery root and shallots into a medium pot, add water to cover and 1 tablespoon salt, and bring to a boil over high heat. Reduce the heat to a simmer and cook until the celery root is tender, 10 to 15 minutes.

Strain out the celery root and shallot, reserving the cooking liquid, then place the vegetables in a blender or food processor and set aside for the moment. Put the butter into the pot you cooked the celery root in. Turn the heat to medium and cook the butter until it just starts to brown. Pay attention to the smell (it's nutty when it browns) and the color (look for small specks of brown appearing on the bottom of the pot). When it has started to brown, typically in 2 to 3 minutes with this small amount of butter, turn off the heat and stir in the rosemary.

Using a spatula, transfer the browned rosemary butter into the blender or food processor with the celery root and shallots. Add the cream, horseradish, and enough reserved cooking water to achieve a consistency you prefer, keeping in mind the cooking liquid is salted. Blend until smooth.

Season to taste, adding a little lemon juice if you want it a bit brighter.

Celery Root and King Trumpet Mushroom Salad
with Pine Nuts and Parmesan

Celery root, with its sweet nuttiness, is a great partner to the earthy, slightly briny king trumpet mushrooms. Fall is the time of year to feature this salad, when you might be mourning the end of tomato season. The addition of sliced celery and celery leaves echoes the connection between common celery and its less common cousin. Use a vegetable peeler to create lovely shavings of the Parmesan cheese.

SERVES 4

Olive oil, as needed

½ pound fresh king trumpet mushrooms

1¼ teaspoons salt, divided

1 pound celery root

2 lemons, divided

1 celery stalk, with leaves

¼ teaspoon crushed red pepper flakes

1 teaspoon porcini powder (see Note; optional)

¼ cup pine nuts, toasted

¼ cup shaved Parmesan cheese

½ cup parsley leaves, for garnish

Preheat the oven to 450°F. Line two baking pans with parchment paper and brush with olive oil.

Trim ⅛ inch off the stem end of the mushrooms and discard. Slice the mushrooms vertically (cap through stem) into ¼-inch thick slices. Lay them out on one of the baking sheets. Brush with more olive oil and sprinkle ½ teaspoon of the salt over the mushrooms.

In a medium bowl of water, squeeze half a lemon and set aside. Cut the peel off the celery root as instructed on page 135. Take three-quarters of the celery root, medium dice, and set aside. Finely julienne the remaining one-quarter and place the julienned celery root into the bowl of lemon water and reserve for garnish. On the other baking sheet, toss the diced celery root with a little more olive oil and season with ½ teaspoon salt. Put both the mushrooms and the celery root baking pans in the oven and roast until both are lightly browned in spots, 15 to 25 minutes. Let cool at room temperature.

continues ➤

Using a mandoline or very sharp knife, cut the celery stalk on the bias into paper-thin slices. Cut any celery leaves into ribbons and reserve for garnish. Using a vegetable peeler, peel 3 or 4 strips off one of the lemons and finely julienne. Reserve for garnish.

In a spice grinder, pulse the red pepper flakes, porcini powder, pine nuts, and the remaining ¼ teaspoon salt until it reaches a chunky consistency.

Arrange the cooked king trumpet slices and roasted celery root on a platter. Sprinkle the cut celery stalk over the top. Drizzle some olive oil on top (1 to 2 teaspoons, but you don't need to measure). Sprinkle the pine nut mixture over the top. Garnish with the cheese shavings, julienned celery root, celery leaves, and parsley leaves. Squeeze some lemon over the top and taste for seasoning.

Note

To make porcini powder (or any mushroom powder), simply finely grind dried mushrooms in a spice grinder. Sprinkle the mushroom powder on onions when you make soups or stews to enrich and deepen flavors, or use in the Furikake (page 151).

Celery Root Gratin *with Gruyère, Fennel, and Coriander*

Lightly spiced cream bathes celery root and potatoes, getting it ready for a hot date with not just one amazing cheese but two. All sorts of mixing and mingling is happening beneath that foil, with the oils from fennel and coriander seeds riveted by the herbal banter from the thyme, the celery root yielding under the heat into meltingly tender discs. Finally, fi-nal-ly, it's time to strip away the foil, expose the gratin to the heat from above, and let it bubble away into a glorious masterpiece of perfect chemistry. Assemble two of these and freeze one, unbaked. You can cook it frozen; just add another thirty minutes to the baking time.

SERVES 4

1 tablespoon unsalted butter, softened
1 tablespoon fennel seeds
1 tablespoon coriander seeds
1 tablespoon black peppercorns
1 cup heavy cream
2 cups whole milk
1 teaspoon salt
1 small shallot, quartered
8 sprigs fresh thyme
⅛ teaspoon freshly grated nutmeg
1 lemon, zested
2 pounds celery root
1 large russet potato (about 10 ounces), peeled
4 ounces Gruyère cheese, grated
2 ounces Parmesan cheese, grated

Preheat the oven to 350°F. Grease a 2-quart baking dish with the butter.

Add the fennel, coriander, and peppercorns to a spice grinder and pulse two to three times to break up lightly (you want it to be rather chunky). In the bottom of a saucepan over medium heat, add the spices and stir around for a minute or two until fragrant. Add the cream, milk, salt, shallot, thyme, and nutmeg to the spices. Bring to a boil, remove from heat, add the lemon zest, cover, and let steep for 15 minutes.

Cut the peel off the celery root as instructed on page 135. Using a mandoline, slice the celery root and potato crosswise into ⅛-inch slices. Strain the milk mixture through a sieve, put the milk back into the saucepan, and add the potatoes and celery root to the hot milk mixture, tossing the potatoes and celery root through it.

Combine the cheeses together in a bowl. Lay the sliced potatoes and celery root in an even layer in the serving dish, then add a sprinkling of cheese. Repeat this until the vegetables and cheese are used up. Pour the remaining milk mixture over the top of the dish. Bake, covered, for 45 minutes. Set the oven to broil, uncover the gratin, and place on the middle rack and broil until the top is brown and bubbly, 5 to 10 minutes. Allow the gratin to rest for at least 30 minutes before serving to allow the dish to set up.

Radish

AKA
RAPHANUS RAPHANISTRUM
SUBSP. SATIVUS, GARDEN
RADISH, RADISH PLANT

THE 411: I'll never forget the time my father handed me a tiny baby radish he had grown in the garden and told me to try it. I couldn't believe how spicy it was. I thought it had to be a chile pepper. I was a kid and sort of gullible, and I got teased a bit, so I'm sure my dad and older brothers told me it was a chile pepper. My dad also had me try Tabasco straight because he knew I would, but that's a story for another time. (Just kidding, Dad! No, not about the Tabasco, you really did that, but about calling you out.) Radishes are a root vegetable in the *Brassica* genus and were domesticated in Asia long before the Romans came on the scene. They are eaten and grown around the world, and they are well known to beginning gardeners as a forgiving crop that grows fast and delivers a mature harvest quickly.

While the most common form of radish in the United States is the small red radish, a tour of a seed catalog or your local farmers' market in the spring reveals a wide world of radishes in every color and shape (see box on page 145). What radishes have in common, no matter the variety, is their tendency to be a cooler weather crop (rarely are they at their best in the summer). Radishes have a range of pepperiness, from just a small amount to a wallop of it. Radishes are good raw, pickled, and cooked, though they are less often cooked in cuisines beyond Japan and Korea (and that is a travesty, as stewed daikon is a sweet, lovely thing). The whole plant is edible including the greens, which are often overlooked as a food source. Radish greens are arugula-like, healthful, and a great addition when cooked into stir-fries and soups. They are also terrific eaten raw, such as when cut into thin ribbons for salads.

Culturally, the daikon radish is a very important root vegetable in Japan, Mexico, and Korea. Radish dolls are created from them (google *daikon doll* and go down a rabbit hole of cuteness overload). In the Japanese Festival of Seven Herbs (*Nanakusa no sekku*), celebrated on the seventh day after the new year, daikon and six other "herbs" are eaten in congee to bring health and longevity. The daikon even plays a part in a Mexican festival where, on December 23, locals in Oaxaca celebrate the Night of the Radishes (*Noche de Rábanos*), when oversized radishes are carved and displayed in the zocalo, or town square.

AKA: *Raphanus raphanistrum* subsp. *sativus,* garden radish, radish plant (the word *radish* comes from the Latin root *radix,* meaning root).

NUTRITION FACTS: Radishes are high in vitamin C and other antioxidants, with lesser amounts of potassium, folate, and vitamin B$_6$.

SEASON: Most radish varieties are at their peak in the spring, though daikon radish has a fall and winter season.

PURCHASE, STORAGE, AND PREP TIPS: No matter the variety, when choosing radishes make sure that the radish is firm—give it a squeeze and choose ones that are solid, resisting the pressure. Good-looking leaves are a great sign of freshness (and they are delicious raw or cooked). Make sure there are no cracks in the radishes and no blemishes. Store radishes in a produce bag in the crisper drawer of your fridge. If you have radishes with their leaves attached, remove the leaves and store them in a separate bag with a dry paper towel wrapped around them. Leaves attached to any root vegetable are water vampires and will take that water from the root if left attached.

COOKING TIPS: Most radishes are used in raw or pickled preparations. Cooking radishes makes the root less pungent and spicy, bringing out a mild, sweeter flavor profile that complements many dishes. When roasting radishes, use high heat for better browning and flavor development. You can roast small radishes whole, but cutting them in half showcases their contrasting interiors. Steaming or blanching and shocking radishes, and then throwing them on the grill to get some smoke flavor in the mix, is an underused technique that I highly recommend. For all cases of cooked radishes, cook them just until they are tender, much like you would cook a potato.

SUBS: Substitute one radish variety for another. But if that's not an option, white turnip is a great substitute, giving you the texture and slight peppery note. Cabbage hearts, jicama, and a tiny bit of grated horseradish can also be used.

How Many Radish Varieties Have You Tried?

Check the boxes below (yes, you can mark up this book, dog-ear pages, and in the best traditions of a cookbook well used, dribble some oil or sauce on it):

☐ Red radish (most common, spicy, red exterior, white interior)

☐ Easter egg (white, purple, pink, or crimson)

☐ French breakfast (ovoid, red and white two-toned exterior, white interior, adorable)

☐ Spanish black (black exterior, white interior)

☐ Watermelon radish (green exterior, pink starburst interior [such a looker!], mild)

☐ Daikon (quite long; more mild than red radishes and sweeter, as well as having more water content; white, green, and purple varieties)

☐ Lobak (closely related to daikon but spicier, used for making Chinese radish cakes)

☐ Mammoth white (*Sakurajima* in Japanese, the largest radish in the world weighed in at 100 pounds, a variety of daikon)

☐ White icicle (slim, long radishes but smaller than daikon)

☐ None (I mistrust radishes, which is why I'm reading this book. Welcome! You've come to the right place.)

This is a mere selection of the variety of radishes that exist. There are many, many more!

Quick Pickled Daikon Radishes
with Turmeric and Lime

These quick pickled radishes can live in your fridge for up to a month. I like serving them on cheese boards or as a funky, acidic accompaniment to Charred Chard with Spicy Chile Oil (page 129), with coconut rice and fried egg; Fried Rice with Burdock, Sesame, and Seaweed (page 29); or Mustard Greens and Spinach with Toasted Sesame Dressing (page 218). The Thai basil is infused into the pickling liquid and then taken out so that the pickle stays fresher and the herbs don't get weird. If you know you're going to eat up the pickle within the week, feel free to leave the basil in the jar—you can even stuff more in the jar if you feel like it.

SERVES 4

1 cup unseasoned rice vinegar

1 cup water

1 teaspoon roughly ground black pepper

¼ cup honey

1 teaspoon turmeric

2 large sprigs Thai basil

Peel of 1 lime

1 pound daikon radish, cut into triangles or any shape you like

In a medium saucepan over high heat bring the rice vinegar, water, black pepper, and honey to a boil. Turn off the heat and whisk in the turmeric. Drop in the Thai basil and lime peel, cover the pot, and let it infuse for 20 minutes. Add the cut daikon radish to a mason jar. Remove the basil from the pickling liquid and pour the liquid over the radish. Let it cool at room temperature and then put the lid on and store in your refrigerator. It's ready to eat right away but gets more flavorful after a few days.

Watermelon Radish "Crostini"
with Onion Dip and Potato-Chive Crunch

Watermelon radish is such a flamboyant stunner, and this recipe shows off its party dress. The idea behind this recipe was to create a one-bite appetizer that takes an unusual vegetable and transforms it into something familiar. Salt and vinegar is a classic combo, whether in chips or fries, and most everyone likes dipping things in onion dip. Bring out the bubbles for this appetizer, or at least The Champagne of Beers (Miller High Life). Or, if you want to be more chill with this dish, simply place the dip in a bowl surrounded by the watermelon radishes and put the potato-chive garnish on top. PS: When you open the jar after pickling the radish, it will release a distinctly farty smell. The smell dissipates. It's the aromatic tax you pay for understanding the misunderstood.

SERVES 4 TO 6

½ pound watermelon radish, peeled
1 cup seasoned rice vinegar
1 tablespoon olive oil
1 onion, small diced
1½ teaspoons salt, divided
1 cup whole fat Greek yogurt
¼ cup of your favorite salted potato chips
2 tablespoons finely sliced chives, dried well on a paper towel

Cut the radish into ⅓-inch rounds. Cut the rounds into halves or quarters. Place in a narrow jar and pour the seasoned rice vinegar over the top. Cover, stick it in the fridge, and let it quick pickle for at least 30 minutes.

Heat a medium sauté pan over medium heat. Add the olive oil, onion, and 1 teaspoon of the salt. Stir well, cover the pan, and turn the heat to low. Set a timer for 10 minutes. Stir when the timer goes off and cover for another 10 minutes. Add a tablespoon of water if the onions are sticking at all. After the second timer goes off, turn the heat to medium-high and, with the cover off, stir from time to time until the onions turn a toasty brown color, about 20 more minutes.

Remove the onions to a blender bowl (or use an immersion blender). Add the Greek yogurt and ½ teaspoon salt. Taste it! Crush up the potato chips with your hands into tiny pieces (if you have children, let them do this, as there are few opportunities to give children permission to be little monsters and this is one of them). Drain the radishes from the pickling liquid and save that liquid to pickle other vegetables (it will have a rosy hue, but it won't stain brightly colored foods). Dry the watermelon radishes off well with towels. Lay them out on a platter.

Use a piping bag or a plastic storage bag with the corner cut off and pipe the onion dip onto the radishes. Combine the crushed chips with the dried chives. Garnish with the potato chip–chive mixture.

Roasted Radishes *with Miso Butter and Furikake*

This recipe is relatively easy, especially if you purchase the furikake instead of making your own. It's super savory with the miso butter. Eat the roasted radishes with rice and roasted or grilled mushrooms, or with a side of the Mustard Greens and Spinach with Toasted Sesame Dressing (page 218). Look in the index for the other recipes in this book that use miso so you can use up the container. Pick the prettiest and smallest radishes you can find for this dish to up the wee factor. Speaking of the wee factor, look closely at the photo on page 151. The radish in the middle is staring back at you.

SERVES 4

FOR THE MISO BUTTER

2 tablespoons unsalted butter, room temperature

1 tablespoon red miso

1 teaspoon lemon zest, more if needed

Salt, if needed

FOR THE ROASTED RADISHES

¾ pound Cherry Belle radishes (typical round red radishes) with tops, if possible

¾ pound French breakfast radishes or another heirloom type, with tops, if possible

¾ pound White Beauty radishes or another heirloom type, with tops, if possible

1 pound small carrots

1 teaspoon Furikake (store-bought or make your own; recipe follows)

Preheat the oven to 450°F. Line two baking sheets with parchment paper.

TO MAKE THE MISO BUTTER

In a small bowl, beat together the butter, miso, and lemon zest with a wooden spoon. You can make it easier on yourself if you'd like and let a stand mixer do the grunt work of combining it. Taste and add salt or lemon zest. Feel free to double or triple this recipe.

TO MAKE THE ROASTED RADISHES

Scrub the radishes and carrots. If the carrots are organic, there is no need to peel them. If the radishes and carrots are very tiny and slender, in the case of the carrot, feel free to leave them whole with an inch or two of the green tops. Cut large radishes in quarters, medium radishes in half, and the teeniest of them can remain whole. Refer to the picture on page 151 for a visual of the sizes. It's important to keep them relatively the same size so they will cook at the same rate.

Place the radishes and carrots on the prepared baking sheets. Using a spatula, transfer the miso butter from the bowl to the sheets with the vegetables. Pop the sheets in the oven for 5 minutes, just until the butter melts. Bring the sheets out of the oven and toss all the vegetables thoroughly now that the butter has melted. Put the sheets back in the oven and roast until the vegetables are caramelized and tender. Cooking time depends on what

size you cut your vegetables. Small radishes will be done in about 15 minutes, larger ones might take 25 minutes. A knife should pierce the vegetables easily with no resistance.

Sprinkle the vegetables with 1 teaspoon of furikake to your taste. Serve right away or at room temperature.

FURIKAKE

1 tablespoon nori flakes (or 1 sheet of nori blitzed in spice grinder)
1 tablespoon white sesame seeds, toasted
1 tablespoon black sesame seeds, toasted
½ teaspoon porcini or shiitake powder (see Note on page 140)

In a small bowl, mix all the ingredients together. Feel free to double, triple, or quadruple this recipe. Store in an airtight container away from light and heat, or in the fridge for longer storage.

Parsnip

THE 411: Parsnip is a nutty, super sweet (when cooked), stealth vegetable that flies under the radar, disguising itself as a large, white, slightly strange-looking carrot. Cultivated by the Romans and native to Eurasia, British colonizers brought it to the United States, where its popularity dwindled in favor of that scene-stealer, the potato. Parsnip is in the Apiaceae family and is related to carrot and parsley. Prior to the widespread use of cane sugar, parsnip was used as a sweetener in Europe. I'll take my coffee with two cubes of parsnip, thank you very much. Interestingly, parsnips don't play a large role in modern Italian cuisine. So where are all the parsnips being eaten in the world? There is no misunderstanding about the parsnip in the United Kingdom, where they hold contests to see who can grow the longest one, and Christmas dinner and traditional Sunday roast would be a disaster without a side of parsnips.

If parsnips are so much like a carrot but sweeter when cooked, reminiscent of potato (one of the world's most beloved tubers), easily pureed into the creamiest of soups without getting gluey like potatoes do, and nutritious to boot, why are parsnips so underused? It seems that when potatoes came on the scene, parsnips were kicked out of bed like they were on fire. I've asked some people because I'm genuinely at a loss. Who, collectively, overcooked parsnips and served mushy, under-seasoned specimens throughout our country so much so that no one really eats them anymore? Have we been parsnip traumatized? What's it going to take, America? Do we need chef and restaurateur Yotam Ottolenghi to go on a state-by-state tour, layering caramelized parsnips on a bed of labneh with mint and pomegranate seeds, for us to finally let the weird white carrot in the party?

AKA: *Pastinaca sativa,* wild parsnip.

NUTRITION FACTS: Parsnips are a good source of fiber, potassium, vitamin K, folate, vitamin C, and other antioxidants.

SEASON: Parsnips are at their best after the first frost in the fall and, like carrots, can be harvested through the winter.

PURCHASE, STORAGE, AND PREP TIPS: Choose parsnips that are on the medium to small size, as these are more tender and less woody. They should be smooth, pale in color, and firm. Avoid any that are soft, limp, or shriveled. Store them just as you would carrots, in a produce bag in the crisper drawer of your fridge. They will keep for about two to three weeks. To prep them, wash them well, trim off the stem end, and peel with a vegetable peeler. If you buy organic or unsprayed parsnips, you can eat the peel. Just cut them up and roast them, and you'll get a bit more nutrition that way. Try it and see what you think. Parsnips, like potatoes, can discolor (oxidize) if you leave them exposed to the air, so cut them right before you're going to cook them. If you're storing cut pieces for later, keep them in water or squeeze a bit of lemon juice on them. That's what I do when I serve young, cut-up parsnips on a vegetable tray. Some people cut out the woody core of the parsnip. I recommend this only if you have purchased a large, older one and you are serving it raw. If you are cooking them, the core will tenderize, unless you bought really old ones (and you should avoid that, in general, unless you plan on pureeing them for a soup).

COOKING TIPS: Parsnips are typically cooked but can be eaten raw as well. Make sure you choose smaller, more tender ones to avoid the fibrous core that develops in larger, more mature roots. Surprise your friends by sneaking some young sticks of parsnip next to the carrots with some dip and see if they notice. When cooking parsnips, avoid overcooking (unless you will be pureeing them into a soup or sauce), as they can become mushy. Parsnips get noticeably sweet after cooking. High heat and shorter cooking times gets you more flavor. And if it chars a little that's OK: some contrasting bitterness from the charring plays well against the sweetness.

SUBS: Carrots are the obvious choice here, as they share the nutty, earthy, sweet vibe. But beyond carrots, reach for turnips, parsley root (if you can find it), and daikon radish.

Parsnip Soup *with Apple Butter and Fried Parsnips*

Who doesn't love a good soup? It's like sauce, but more. While the addition of the home-made apple butter and the home-fried parsnip chips escorts this soup into the fancy chef party, no one will know if you buy apple butter and root vegetable chips at the store. So there you go: you have permission to take this more difficult recipe and turn it into a week-night thing that's still damn impressive. If you do end up going the make-it-all-yourself route, the nice thing about the parsnips roasting away for 30 minutes is that it gives you the time to make the apple butter and chips.

SERVES 4

- 3 pounds parsnips, cut 2⅔ pounds into large chunks (reserve ⅓ pound uncut parsnips for making the optional chips; recipe follows)
- 1 large onion, cut into wedges
- 3 tablespoons olive oil
- 1 teaspoon truffle salt, more if needed
- 1 teaspoon salt
- ½ teaspoon freshly ground black pepper
- ½ cup dry white vermouth (or dry white wine)
- 8 cups vegetable stock (or use water), more if needed
- 2 bay leaves
- 1 lemon, juiced
- Homemade apple butter, for garnish (recipe follows; or use purchased apple butter)
- Parsnip chips, for garnish (recipe follows; optional)

Preheat the oven to 400°F. Line a baking sheet with parchment paper.

Place the parsnips and onion on the sheet and toss with the olive oil, truffle salt, regular salt, and pepper. Roast in the oven until browned and tender, approximately 30 minutes, then set aside.

Add the cooked vegetables to a medium saucepot along with the vermouth, vegetable stock, and bay leaves. Bring to a boil, reduce to a simmer, and cook for 15 minutes.

Puree the soup in a blender until it is silky smooth. Thin, if necessary, with more stock or water. Add the lemon juice as needed to brighten the soup and season to taste with more truffle salt.

Serve the soup with a spoonful of apple butter and a few parsnip chips.

continues ➡

APPLE BUTTER

3 apples (different types make for a more
  interesting butter), cored
1 cup unsweetened apple cider
¼ teaspoon salt
1 teaspoon ground cinnamon

Cut the apples into chunks with the skins still on and place them in a saucepan. Add the apple cider, salt, and cinnamon and cook for about 30 minutes, with the lid on, over medium-low heat until the apples have broken down. Stir from time to time and make sure it doesn't stick to the bottom of the pan or burn.

Press the apples through a fine mesh sieve (or put through a food mill), then discard the apple skins. Reduce the apple butter in a saucepan over low heat, lid off, until it is thick (30 to 40 minutes more). It should be sweet enough without any added sweetener.

PARSNIP CHIPS

These can be made ahead of time. When cool, store in an airtight container at room temperature for a few days.

SERVES 4

2 cups high-heat oil
⅓ pound parsnips (reserved from soup),
  peeled and then sliced into thin strips
Salt, as needed

Heat the oil in a saucepan to 350°F. Drop batches of the parsnips into the oil and, moving them gently around as they fry, cook until the parsnip chips are golden brown, about 1 to 2 minutes. Immediately remove to paper towels to drain off excess fat, then season to taste with salt.

Farro and Parsnip Salad *with Persimmon, Celery, and Almonds*

When the leaves are falling and parsnips and persimmons hit the produce section of your supermarket, it's time to make this super satisfying salad (if you can't find persimmons, head to an Asian grocery store if you live near one, or substitute with a mixture of sungold tomatoes and plums). You can eat this salad for lunch on its own, as it's surprisingly filling. The interplay of the farro and parsnip hits all the right earthy, nutty notes, and the beguiling melon-meets-mango/passionfruit flavor of the persimmon plays the perfect culinary foil. The almonds give the salad little bursts of salt and crunch. This salad keeps well and can be eaten for several days after you make it. Make sure you buy the right variety of persimmon. You want fuyu, which are eaten when they are still firm, like an apple. The other common persimmon variety, hachiya, is eaten when it's almost oozy soft—if it's eaten any sooner, the tannins suck all the moisture out of your mouth. Let's just say I learned that the hard way.

SERVES 4

FOR THE BALSAMIC VINAIGRETTE
1 cup olive oil
½ cup white balsamic vinegar
1 teaspoon maple syrup or honey
½ teaspoon salt
¼ teaspoon freshly ground black pepper

FOR THE SALAD
1 pound whole farro (order from Bluebird Grain Farms online if you can't find it locally)
2 quarts water
1 tablespoon salt, divided, to taste
1½ pounds parsnips, peeled and medium diced
3 stalks celery, thinly sliced on the bias
1 cup Marcona almonds, roughly chopped
½ cup dried currants
3 fuyu persimmons, peeled and small diced
½ cup chopped parsley, divided

Preheat the oven to 400°F. Line a baking sheet with parchment paper.

TO MAKE THE VINAIGRETTE
Combine all the vinaigrette ingredients together in a jar, shake well, taste, and adjust according to your preference.

TO MAKE THE SALAD
Rinse and drain the farro and then place in a medium pot along with the 2 quarts of water. Add 2 teaspoons of the salt, bring to a boil, reduce to a simmer, and cook for 35 to 40 minutes. Taste. It should be chewy, nearly bouncy in texture, but not hard or crunchy. Drain well and let cool.

Meanwhile, place the parsnips on the baking sheet. Drizzle 2 tablespoons of the vinaigrette over the parsnips and roast in the oven until caramelized and tender, 15 to 20 minutes.

When the parsnips and farro are cool, combine them in a large bowl along with the celery, almonds, currants, persimmons, and half of the parsley. Pour the dressing over the top. Gently mix. Taste for seasoning and adjust, if necessary. Transfer to a serving bowl and garnish with the rest of the parsley.

Chile and Honey-Glazed Roasted Parsnips and Carrots

Not only is this recipe easy on the eyes and simple to make, it packs in some surprising complexity. The ancho chile offers a nice bright smokiness with a hint of fruit that both accentuates the earthiness of the parsnips and brightens it. Adding the vinegar after the cooking keeps it from being lost in the mix and balances the sweetness of the caramelized honey-drizzled vegetables. This recipe would pair well with a mushroom bourguignon or even braised greens and beans.

SERVES 4

1 pound parsnips
1 pound carrots
¼ cup olive oil
1 teaspoon ancho chile powder
½ teaspoon salt
2 tablespoons honey
1 tablespoon white wine vinegar
¼ cup chopped parsley

Preheat the oven to 450°F. Line a baking sheet with parchment paper.

Peel or scrub the parsnips and carrots. If they are organic there is no need to peel them. If they are small, feel free to leave them whole with a little of the green top. If they are bigger, you can split them lengthwise and cut them in half or into whatever shape you like.

Toss the veg with the olive oil, then spread out onto the baking sheet. They shouldn't overlap. Sprinkle the chile powder and salt over the top. If your honey isn't pourable, heat it up in a small saucepot or in the microwave. Drizzle the honey over the veg. Roast until the parsnips and carrots are caramelized and a knife slips in and out easily, anywhere from 15 to 30 minutes depending on the size. As soon as the vegetables are done, drizzle the vinegar over the top, mix well, and top with the parsley. Serve right away or at room temperature.

Romanesco

AKA

BRASSICA OLERACEA
'ROMANESCO', ROMAN
CAULIFLOWER, ROMANESCO
CAULIFLOWER, BROCCOLO
ROMANESCO, ROMANESCO
BROCCOLI, BROCCOFLOWER

THE 411: Romanesco, in my eyes, is one of the most beautiful vegetables to grace our planet. It's also the mathematical nerd's veggie of choice. Each chartreuse bud winds around in seemingly endless patterns, forming what is known in mathematics as a Fibonacci sequence. Math has never been more delicious! Romanesco is a slightly sweet member of the *Brassica* genus, and it tastes somewhat like a cross between broccoli and cauliflower, yet firmer with its own unique nuttiness.

There is little information about the origins of romanesco, save that it was first documented in Italy in the 16th century. Beyond this, there is a surprising lack of information about romanesco that is accessible in English, leading many to conclude, naturally, that its appearance on our planet was seeded by aliens.

Much of the misunderstanding about romanesco has to do with its appearance and similarity to cauliflower and broccoli. Is it cauliflower? Is it broccoli? (If I eat it, will an alien probe be implanted in my stomach?) It's a cousin of cauliflower and broccoli but not a variety of either. Making it as clear as mud, the common names for our fractal friend use both cauliflower and broccoli. Confusion about names aside, there are few vegetables that pack so much nutritional value into such a unique package. When you see it at the supermarket, grab it!

AKA: *Brassica oleracea 'Romanesco,'* Roman cauliflower, romanesco cauliflower, broccolo romanesco, romanesco broccoli, broccoflower.

NUTRITION FACTS: Romanesco is high in dietary fiber, vitamin K, carotenoids, and vitamin C.

SEASON: A cool-weather crop, look for romanesco to be at its peak in the fall, with its season extending into the winter and early spring.

PURCHASE, STORAGE, AND PREP TIPS: Look for firm, heavy heads. A sure sign of freshness is if you see fresh leaves still attached. Keep it in a produce bag in your crisper drawer and make sure to wash it just before you use it to avoid moisture-related mold issues. As with most produce, too much moisture trapped in a humid bag hastens rotting. It will be at its best within a week of purchase. All parts are edible; just remove any dark bits, wilted leaves, and dried-out parts where it was cut off from the plant.

COOKING TIPS: Most importantly, don't overcook romanesco, as it can get mushy. It can be blanched in salted boiling water and shocked in cold water; it can be steamed and added to salads; or it can be roasted at high temperatures, which, like with most foods, brings out more depth of flavor. It can be pickled, or it can be coated in flour (try chickpea flour) and pan- or deep-fried. It can also be sliced thin and eaten raw, maybe coated lightly with a vinaigrette.

SUBS: Broccoli or cauliflower.

Romanesco Steaks *with Lemon-Sesame Dressing and Basil*

When cut into steaks, romanesco takes on a satisfyingly toothsome texture that makes this dish quite hearty. To round out the dish, cook up some brown rice or farro. When you're cutting the romanesco into steaks, some small florets inevitably break off. No worries about that at all. Simply roast up the smaller pieces alongside the steaks. Just keep an eye on them, as they will likely cook a little faster. A large romanesco gets you about four "steaks" that stay intact. I typically buy two heads when I want to make this to up my chances of getting one nice "steak" per person. I use the leftovers for another dish.

SERVES 4

FOR THE LEMON-SESAME DRESSING
½ cup full-fat yogurt
1 teaspoon salt
½ teaspoon black pepper
1 tablespoon tahini
Juice and zest of 2 Meyer lemons
1 teaspoon honey
1 teaspoon sesame oil
1 teaspoon gluten-free tamari (or soy sauce)
1 tablespoon seasoned rice vinegar
¼ cup olive oil
¼ cup safflower oil

FOR THE ROMANESCO STEAKS
2 smaller heads romanesco
½ cup basil leaves, roughly torn or chopped (small leaves can remain whole), for garnish
1 tablespoon sumac, for garnish (optional)

Preheat the oven to 400°F. Line a baking sheet with parchment paper.

TO MAKE THE DRESSING
Using an immersion blender or whisk, combine the yogurt, salt, pepper, tahini, lemon zest, lemon juice, honey, sesame oil, tamari, and rice vinegar. With the blender running or you whisking, slowly add both oils. Taste; it should be quite bright and lemony.

TO MAKE THE ROMANESCO STEAKS
Trim the stem end of the romanesco, then, with the stem on the cutting board, cut vertical ½-inch slices (steaks). Do this carefully to try to keep the slices together. Trim off the sides on the first and last cuts so they sit flat on the pan. Don't worry if some florets break off. Lay the romanesco steaks on the parchment paper. Brush or drizzle one-half of the dressing over the romanesco, carefully turning the steaks over to get well coated.

Roast in the oven until well caramelized and tender, 15 to 25 minutes. Serve warm or at room temperature with more dressing drizzled over the top. Garnish with the basil leaves and sumac, if using.

Roasted Romanesco Rice
with Jalapeño, Lime, and Cilantro

Carbs are the reason I wake up in the morning, and on good days carbs are the last thing I see before I go to bed. It might appear from the title of this recipe that I'm jumping on the latest food or diet trend, though in truth I developed it out of pure curiosity. Admittedly, for sure I am following trends in the recipe for Buffalo-Style Roasted Romanesco (page 168)—I can't help it; it's just stupid delicious. Back to my curiosity: what would it taste like if I grated romanesco, dry-brined it (salted it heavily), got the moisture out to concentrate the flavor, and then added some bold seasonings plus high heat? Again, stupid delicious. More flavorful than cauliflower rice, more interesting than white rice, and sure, far fewer carbs . . . but that's beside the point. Serve this in place of any rice dish, in tacos, as a side dish with eggs and refried beans, or just eat it out of the pan the way I did.

SERVES 4

1 pound romanesco (about 1 medium head)

1 teaspoon salt

2 tablespoons high-heat oil

¼ teaspoon chipotle powder, plus more to taste

1 bunch cilantro, leaves chopped and reserved for garnish, stems finely chopped

1 jalapeño, seeds and membranes removed, minced

1 lime, zested and juiced

Preheat the oven to 500°F. Line a baking sheet with parchment paper (fold under the paper on the pan so it doesn't hang over the edge).

Using the grater attachment on a food processor, finely chop up the romanesco, or grate by hand on the large side of a box grater. In a large bowl, toss the romanesco with the salt and let it sit for 15 minutes. After 15 minutes, gently squeeze the romanesco over the sink, squeezing out any water.

Toss the romanesco with the oil, chipotle powder, cilantro stems, and jalapeño. Roast for 15 minutes, until lightly browned. Scrape into a bowl and toss with the lime zest, lime juice, and cilantro leaves.

Buffalo-Style Roasted Romanesco

Everything I love about Buffalo chicken wings is intact in this recipe: the spicy-sweet, buttery sauce, the crunch, even the meaty texture. The first key to this recipe is in making sure the roasted coating on the romanesco is quite crunchy before you call it done. Make sure to carefully touch one to see that it is crispy all over. If not, back in it goes. The second key is that you must eat them right away, before the steam inside the romanesco makes the coating soft. Think of them as you would fries. Cauliflower works great in this recipe as a substitute.

SERVES 4

1 large head romanesco (about 1¼ pounds)
¾ cup flour
1 teaspoon salt
¼ teaspoon freshly ground black pepper
1 teaspoon smoked paprika
¾ to 1 cup buttermilk
¼ cup Frank's RedHot sauce
2 tablespoons unsalted butter
2 ounces blue cheese crumbles,
  for garnish

Preheat the oven to 400°F. Line two baking sheets with parchment paper, making sure the paper does not extend over the edge.

Wash the romanesco, dry it well, trim the stem end, core the romanesco, and cut the core into bite-sized pieces. Cut the rest of it into bite-sized florets. In a large bowl, whisk up the flour, salt, pepper, and smoked paprika. Add the buttermilk, starting with ¾ cup, and whisk well. It should be the consistency of thick pancake batter or Greek yogurt. Add up to 1 cup if needed. You want just enough liquid in the batter so that it coats the romanesco, but it should not be runny at all. Add the romanesco to the batter and coat each piece fully by using your hands and tossing it all together so the batter gets in all the nooks and crannies.

Lay the pieces on the baking sheets, leaving a little space between them. Wash your hands because, wow, you're a mess now. Bake for 20 minutes. Flip the pieces over and bake for another 15 to 25 minutes, until they are crispy and golden. While they bake, heat the hot sauce and butter together until the butter melts. Transfer the hot sauce–butter mixture into the bottom of a big bowl.

When the romanesco is done, add it to the bowl with the sauce. Quickly toss them around to get them coated in the sauce, then remove to a platter. Garnish with blue cheese crumbles and serve right away.

Sunchokes

AKA
HELIANTHUS TUBEROSUS,
JERUSALEM ARTICHOKE,
FRENCH OR CANADA
POTATO, CANADIAN TRUFFLE,
LAMBCHOKE, EARTH APPLE,
TOPINAMBOUR, SUNROOT

THE 411: First cultivated by Indigenous Americans, sunchokes resemble large gingerroots. They can be pale brown, white, or even red or purple. They are tubers that grow on the underground rhizomes of a plant that produces beautiful yellow flowers. Now that we have the basics covered, it's time for some hard-hitting honesty. I almost didn't include sunchokes in this book because I had an "incident" with them whereby I ate too many at one sitting and soon learned exactly why they are known as "fartichokes." I'll spare you the details, but please know that I was at a retreat with lots of people, sharing a room, and I had to do some public speaking. Why, I asked myself, would I want to promote a socially awkward, controversially explosive tuber? English botanist John Goodyer wrote about the food in 1621, observing:

Which way soever they be dressed and eaten, they stir and cause a filthy loathsome stinking wind within the body, thereby causing the belly to be pained and tormented, and are a meat more fit for swine than men.

Are sunchokes misunderstood? No, I thought, I understand them very, very well.

But I'm not a quitter, and I soon learned that lots of foods contain inulin (the sugar that feeds your gut bacteria so efficiently that they have a rager of a party in your colon). All of these inulin-containing foods (asparagus, leeks, garlic, dandelion greens) are good for us, but like all good things, eaters should be aware of the amounts they consume in one sitting lest there be consequences. Mileage varies by individual, but I recommend eating no more sunchokes in a sitting than you would beans to see how your body responds. The other reason to eat sunchokes? They are sweet, nutty, and versatile (you can eat them raw or cooked).

AKA: *Helianthus tuberosus* (botanically related to artichokes but not an artichoke), Jerusalem artichoke (it may have gotten the Jerusalem portion of its name from a mispronunciation of the Italian for sunflower (*girasole*) and the fact that the flavor resembles that of an artichoke). Other names include French or Canada potato, Canadian truffle, lambchoke (poor lambs!), earth apple, *topinambour* (German), sunroot.

NUTRITION FACTS: Sunchokes are super nutritious, being high in potassium, iron, calcium, and magnesium. They are high in fiber (duh) and low in carbohydrates. Inulin can help keep blood and glucose levels stable. Have I mentioned they are super high in fiber?

SEASON: At its best in the fall and also in the spring.

PURCHASE, STORAGE, AND PREP TIPS: Look for firm specimens, with no soft or black spots. Sunchokes don't last long in storage. Keep them in paper bags in a cool, dark place or in a produce bag in your fridge. Use them up within a few weeks. Wash them right before you are going to use them to avoid moisture-related mold issues. Sunchokes are knobby, making peeling their thin skins a frustrating process that is completely unnecessary. Scrub them well to get rid of surface dirt and you're good to go.

COOKING TIPS: First of all, you don't even need to cook them. Cut them thin with a knife or mandoline and add to salads, or cut into sticks for dipping in things such as "Beetmus" with Pistachio Dukkah (page 111) or Creamy Artichoke and Miso Dip (page 57). Keep in mind that when cooking sunchokes, the inulin can make them go mushy, so be very careful to not overcook them, especially when boiling. I find that roasting or grilling accentuates their nutty flavor.

SUBS: Artichokes, water chestnuts, and jicama will get you close to the flavor and texture of sunchokes. Despite being different in flavor and texture, romanesco, cauliflower, and potatoes are adequate substitutes for the sunchoke recipes in this book.

Sunchoke and Leek Pot Pie
with Hard Apple Cider and Herbs

Buy frozen puff pastry and follow the thawing instructions, as you will need to plan ahead with this recipe. (It bugs me when you're craving a recipe and you find out too late you had to thaw something out overnight or for multiple hours.) Now back to your regularly scheduled headnote. This is no revelation, but did you know that butter and flour plus time and heat and tasty vegetables are comforting and nurturing? Did you know that you'll want someone to tuck you into it, pulling the pastry over you like a cuddly, buttery blanket so you can nibble sunchokes and sip hard cider and drift into a sweet, sweet slumber? No? Now you do. Wear your pajamas before making this recipe.

SERVES 4

1 package frozen puff pastry, thawed

2 carrots, large diced

1 pound sunchokes, scrubbed and large diced

2 tablespoons olive oil

2 teaspoons salt, divided

3 tablespoons unsalted butter

1 large leek, dark green parts trimmed, light green and white parts small diced

1 shallot, minced

1 stalk celery, small diced

⅛ teaspoon freshly ground black pepper

3 garlic cloves, minced

½ cup hard apple cider (or dry white vermouth and a splash of brandy if you have some)

3 tablespoons flour, plus more for dusting

1 cup cream

1 teaspoon seedy mustard

1 cup vegetable stock

½ cup apple, unpeeled, medium diced

½ bunch lacinato kale, ribs discarded, leaves cut into bite-sized pieces

½ cup chopped fresh herbs (mixture of parsley, dill, sage, thyme, and rosemary)

4 ounces roasted chestnuts, small diced (optional)

1 teaspoon white wine vinegar

1 egg

1 tablespoon milk (or water)

Thaw out the puff pastry according to the directions on the package.

Preheat the oven to 425°F. Line a baking sheet with parchment paper.

Place the carrots and sunchokes on the baking sheet. Toss with the oil, spread out, and season with 1 teaspoon of the salt. Roast in the oven for 20 minutes, until lightly browned and just tender (they will continue to cook in the pot pie).

Meanwhile, heat the butter in a large skillet over medium-high heat. Add the leeks, shallot, celery, 1 teaspoon salt, and the black pepper and sauté for 8 to 10 minutes, until translucent and tender. Add the garlic and

continues ➤

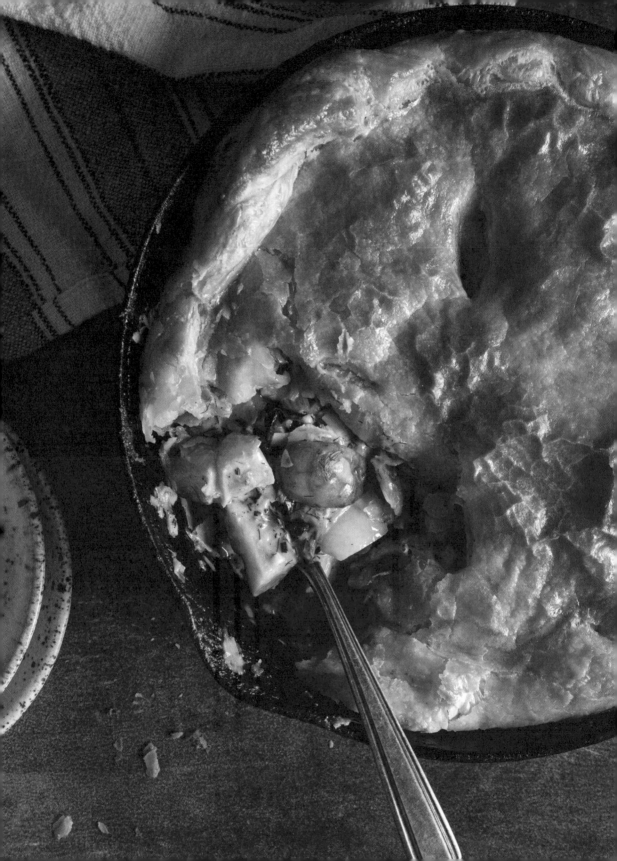

cook for 30 seconds more. Deglaze with the hard cider. Cook until the cider is nearly gone then sprinkle the flour over the mixture, and stir well. Cook for 2 to 3 minutes, stirring frequently. Add the cream, mustard, and stock to the skillet, whisking occasionally until the mixture starts to thicken, 5 to 7 minutes. Once it thickens, add the apple, kale, fresh herbs, optional chestnuts, vinegar, and roasted sunchokes and carrots. Mix everything together well and set aside, off the heat. Let the skillet cool down a bit.

Once the skillet has cooled, take the thawed puff pastry out of the fridge. Working quickly, dust the counter with a little flour and roll the pastry so it will fit over the skillet and hang over by at least 1 to 2 inches. Carefully lay the pastry over the skillet. Fold the overhanging pastry back onto itself to create a dog-eared paper look (refer to the picture on page 174). Whisk the egg with the milk and brush it over the whole surface of the pastry. Finally, cut at least three 1- to 2-inch vents into the pastry.

Pop the skillet onto the parchment paper–lined baking sheet you used earlier for the sunchokes and place in the oven on the middle rack. Set a timer for 20 minutes. When the timer goes off, turn down the heat to 375°F and cook for another 10 minutes, or until the top is puffed and brown and the filling is bubbling through the vents.

Let cool and serve, in bed, so you can fall asleep without having to move.

Roasted Salt and Vinegar Sunchokes
and Potatoes *with Rosemary*

Somewhere between fries and chips are these superthin smoky roasted tubers. This recipe is where you should start your exploration of sunchokes, as you'll get to directly compare the nutty, earthy-sweet flavor of sunchokes in a head-to-head taste-off with the common potato. You can certainly cut these by hand, but this recipe is extra simple if you use a mandoline. I prefer the less expensive Japanese mandolines (Benriner is a brand I like). Make sure to use the hand guard lest you de-veganize the recipe with your own contributions. When you lay the slices out on the pans, it's important that the potatoes and sunchokes don't overlap. If you don't have enough pans, cook in batches or halve the recipe. If you have newspapers around, it's fun to serve them up on the newspaper (see page 177) with plenty of cold beer. Oh, and you should play some cards. Five Crowns is my new favorite card game, and my friend and I played it while eating this entire recipe that is supposed to yield four servings (I never learn). They don't keep very well, but I doubt you'll have an issue with leftovers.

SERVES 4

1 pound sunchokes, scrubbed
¼ cup olive oil, divided
2 tablespoons apple cider vinegar, divided
1 tablespoon smoked salt, divided
1 pound Yukon Gold potatoes
1 tablespoon minced rosemary

Preheat the oven to 450°F. Line two baking sheets with parchment paper.

Using a mandoline, slice the sunchokes into ⅛-inch slices. Lay them on one of the baking sheets. Drizzle 2 tablespoons of the olive oil and 1 tablespoon of the apple cider vinegar over the top. Toss with your hands and then spread them out in a single layer. Sprinkle 1½ teaspoons of the smoked salt on top. Do the same procedure with the potatoes, putting them on the other baking sheet.

Roast for 15 minutes, sprinkle 1½ teaspoons of the minced rosemary over each tray, and roast 5 minutes more, or until the potatoes and sunchokes are crispy (keep in mind they crisp a little upon cooling). Mix the chips together and serve right away.

Smashed Sunchokes *with Soy Caramel Glaze and Green Apple*

Soy caramel, a luscious, umami-packed, buttery teriyaki sauce derivative greater than the sum of its parts, would make a box of rocks taste delicious. I encourage you to pair it with everything from your elbow to said box of rocks. Nutty, earthy sunchokes, when smashed and charred a bit in a cast-iron skillet, pair beautifully with the soy glaze, the richness cut by the tart green apple on top. You can eat this dish on its own along with other vegetable dishes, or you can combine the apples and sunchokes with rice, tuck the mixture into lettuce cups, and dip them in any extra sauce.

SERVES 4

1 pound sunchokes, scrubbed

2 tablespoons salt, plus more to taste

½ Granny Smith apple, unpeeled, julienned

1 tablespoon toasted black sesame seeds

1 small jalapeño, seeded and minced (optional)

1 lemon

1 tablespoon high-heat oil

Soy caramel glaze (recipe follows)

4 cups cooked jasmine or sushi rice (optional)

1 head butter lettuce, for cups (optional)

Place the sunchokes in a medium pot and cover with water by a few inches. Season the water with the salt. Bring the water to a boil and then reduce to a simmer. Cook until the sunchokes can be pierced easily with a knife. Be careful not to overcook them; it should take 10 to 12 minutes.

Drain the sunchokes and let them cool off a bit. Using the bottom of a mason jar, skillet, or other smashing tool of your dreams, gently squish down on each sunchoke to flatten it, being careful not to take out your com-pletely understandable anger with the latest news cycle on the poor defenseless sun-choke. You want the sunchokes to remain in one piece but be flattened to approximately ½ inch to ¾ inch in height.

In a small bowl, mix the apples with the black sesame seeds, optional jalapeño, a squeeze of lemon, and a pinch of salt. Set aside.

Heat the oil over medium-high heat in a large cast-iron skillet (or other heavy-bottomed skillet). After a few moments add the sunchokes in a single layer. Brown well on one side and flip over after a few minutes. Brown on the other side and then turn the heat down to low. Wait a minute for the pan to cool down and then add the soy caramel glaze, tilting the pan and using a spoon, to baste this deliciousness over the sunchokes, glazing them with the sauce. After a minute or so, when the sunchokes are shiny and well glazed, carefully remove them to a platter with a spatula.

Garnish the sunchokes with the apple

mixture. Drizzle any remaining glaze over the top. Serve immediately. If you end up making the rice, simply serve the sunchokes and apple mixture on top of the rice. And if you want to use lettuce cups, wash and dry the lettuce and trim off any less-than-gorgeous bits, stuff a little rice in the concave part of the "cup," top with sunchokes, and drizzle any extra sauce on top. Gather the edges of the cup and voila!

SOY CARAMEL GLAZE

The reduction (all the ingredients before the butter is added) can be made several weeks in advance and kept in the fridge. Warm up and whisk in the butter right before you need it. You can keep the emulsified butter sauce in a preheated thermos for up to two hours. This sauce doubles easily. If the butter solidifies, simply rewarm and blend to re-emulsify.

MAKES ABOUT ½ CUP

2 tablespoons gluten-free tamari sauce (or soy sauce)

¼ cup sake

3 tablespoons mirin

1 teaspoon sugar

1 tablespoon lemon juice, plus more to taste

¼ cup (½ stick) cold unsalted butter, cut into tablespoons

In a small saucepan, add the tamari, sake, mirin, sugar, and lemon juice. Bring to a boil over high heat, then lower the heat and reduce to a simmer. Cook the sauce until it is reduced by half, 5 to 7 minutes (from roughly ¾ cup to about ⅓ cup).

Turn down the heat to its lowest setting and whisk in the butter 1 tablespoon at a time, adding each only after the previous one has melted, or you can emulsify the butter into the warm reduction (without waiting between butter additions), using an immersion blender. Taste and add more lemon juice if desired.

Winter

Cabbage

AKA

GREEN, RED, SAVOY, TAIWANESE CABBAGE: ALL BRASSICA OLERACEA VARIETIES, CANNONBALL CABBAGE (GREEN). NAPA CABBAGE: BRASSICA RAPA SUBSP. PEKINENSIS, CHINESE CABBAGE, WOMBOK

THE 411: Cabbage has been around since before the Middle Ages. The Romans recorded it as a luxury of the table (they're not wrong). Savoy cabbage, on the other hand, is a relative newcomer and downright modern, having been developed in the 16th century. Cabbage is a key ingredient in the cuisines of eastern, central, and northern European countries. Cabbage was brought to Asia, the Americas, and the world at large starting in the early modern era (1500–1700). Napa cabbage originated in China and is extremely popular in East Asian cuisine, so it's no surprise that China is the leading producer of cabbage and other brassicas.

Cabbage is misunderstood in that, for many Americans, it is thought of in a fairly limited sense. If you're Irish, perhaps you cook cabbage on St. Paddy's Day, but generally speaking, the majority of Americans, especially white Americans who do not have eastern European roots, still think of cabbage as the coleslaw vegetable. That way of thinking needs to change (insert picture of cabbage holding a picket sign that says RESPECT ME). Cabbage is extremely versatile and can be eaten raw, cooked, fermented, pickled, used as wrappers, or featured on vegetable platters. It's sweet, crunchy (red and green cabbage), excellent in salads, and beautifully tender and sweet when braised. It's inexpensive. It lasts a very long time in your fridge, especially the red and green varieties. It's the primary ingredient in kimchi, a Korean dish that has become popular across cultural groups. Also try this sometime: Coat red and green cabbage leaves with olive oil, sprinkle with salt, and grill until charred and wilted. Cut into ribbons and squeeze lime over the top. Amazing. It's so much more than slaw.

AKA:

GREEN, RED, SAVOY, TAIWANESE CABBAGE: All *Brassica oleracea* varieties, cannonball cabbage (green).

NAPA CABBAGE: *Brassica rapa* subsp. *pekinensis,* Chinese cabbage, wombok (Australia).

NUTRITION FACTS: Cabbages are a good source of folate, potassium, vitamin K, and fiber. Red cabbage has 10 times as much vitamin A as green cabbage, while green cabbage has slightly more vitamin K than red.

SEASON: Cabbage is a cold-weather vegetable and is in season in the winter, though it's easily found year-round.

PURCHASE, STORAGE, AND PREP TIPS: For all cabbage varieties, make sure that the leaves are plump, free of holes and cut marks, and do not have brown or damaged spots. Especially with the red and green cabbages—they should feel heavy for their size and be tightly compacted. Napa, Taiwanese, and savoy cabbages don't last as long as red and green cabbage, so use those types within a week of purchase and store in bags in the crisper drawer of your fridge. For red and green cabbage, you can easily get a month of service out of them, especially if you are comfortable simply cutting off the oxidized bit where you previously cut off a portion. Even when well-wrapped it seems that cabbage tends to discolor a bit where you cut into it. I just trim and proceed, and my fridge is never without red or green cabbage. When you're ready to cut into the cabbage, first remove any withered outer leaves. Rinse the cabbage and then cut as necessary for your recipe. Remember to eat the cabbage cores—they can be finely shredded and used in any raw preparation, roasted and eaten as you would broccoli stem, or cooked and pureed in vegetable soups.

COOKING TIPS: While you can certainly steam, boil, and microwave cabbage, my go-tos are braising (browning in a pan, adding a flavorful liquid, and then low-heat cooking), roasting, sautéing, and grilling for the very same reasons I've talked about with every vegetable in this book: *flavor!* Caramelization equates to greater flavor development, mitigation of bitterness, and an increase in natural sweetness.

SUBS: Any variety of cabbage can step in for any other variety of cabbage, and that should be your first move if you can't find the specific variety you are looking for. Cabbage is easy to find all over the country. Beyond cabbage, if you had to substitute for a different vegetable entirely, I'd use kohlrabi or Brussels sprouts.

How Many Types of Cabbage Have You Tried?

☐ **Green:** This is the variety that most of us in the United States think of when we think of cabbage: large, round, dense, heavy, and firm leaves. (There is a variety of green cabbage called pointed cabbage, which as the name would imply comes to a point at one end. Pointed cabbage is in season in the summer to early fall, unlike the other cabbages, and is more delicate.)

☐ **Red:** For reasons I don't fully understand, green cabbage is more popular than red. Personally I love making red sauerkraut because you hardly ever see it and I appreciate the pop of color. Red and green are interchangeable in terms of texture and flavor. Red cabbage is red (actually purple) due to anthocyanins (soluble pigments). When in neutral substances (pH-wise), such as water, red cabbage appears purple, but when acid hits red cabbage it turns fuchsia. I usually add an acidic ingredient to red cabbage to lift the color when I cook it, as without an acidic addition the cooking process itself turns the cabbage from blue to blue-gray.

☐ **Savoy:** With dark green, crinkled leaves, savoy cabbage is not as crisp as green or red cabbage, so it's best roasted or sautéed. Savoy cabbage is also more mild than red or green and is beautiful when used for stuffed cabbage. It has a shorter shelf life than the others, so use it within a few days.

☐ **Taiwanese:** This cabbage looks like a green cabbage dropped off the top of a seven-story building. It's flat, has a looser leaf structure, and is notably sweet with a tender texture. I love using this variety for stir-fries. Look for it at Asian markets.

☐ **Napa:** Napa cabbage, which is more closely related to bok choy and turnips than to the other cabbages profiled in this chapter, is often aligned with cabbages in a cook's mind. That's why I've included Napa here. It is oblong instead of round and is more mild in flavor than red or green cabbage. It has tender leaves and is typically eaten raw, fermented into kimchi, or stuffed into dumplings.

Char-Fried Cabbage *with Ginger and Sesame*

The humble cabbage becomes something exalted in this quick dish. At its best, cabbage is silky, buttery goodness with a hint of sweetness and the perfect landing pad for ample quantities of spicy chile oil. If you keep a vat of the oil in the fridge as I do, this dish is ready in under 30 minutes—add a fried egg on top along with rice, and this side dish becomes dinner. Spending the time, using high enough heat, and resisting the urge to constantly stir the food helps set the charred flavor that really makes this dish.

SERVES 4

- 2 pounds Taiwanese cabbage (or green cabbage)
- 2 tablespoons high-heat oil
- 1 teaspoon salt, plus more to taste
- 2 tablespoons julienned ginger
- 1 tablespoon Spicy Chile Oil (recipe follows, or use store-bought chile oil or chile crisp), plus more for serving
- 1 tablespoon gluten-free tamari (or soy sauce)
- 1 tablespoon sesame seeds, toasted
- 1 tablespoon seasoned rice vinegar
- Cooked rice, for serving

Cut the cabbage in quarters. Cut the core pieces out and finely chop. Slice the rest of the cabbage into bite-sized pieces.

Heat a wok or large sauté pan over high heat. Add the oil and, 30 seconds later, one-half of the cabbage and ½ teaspoon of the salt. Cook, tossing only occasionally, until the cabbage gets charred around the edges, 3 to 4 minutes. Set aside and repeat with the second half. Once done, add the reserved sautéed cabbage to the wok. Add the ginger and cook for another 1 to 2 minutes. Add the chile oil, tamari, sesame seeds, and rice vinegar. Cook for a minute longer, then taste and adjust seasonings. Serve with rice and extra chile oil.

continues ➡

SPICY CHILE OIL

You can find many varieties of bottled chile oil in Asian markets or online, but it's ridiculously easy to make a batch from scratch and store it in your fridge. Plus, your homemade oil contains none of the additives and preservatives that are commonly found in the bottled versions. For a mildly spicy version, use 3 tablespoons of red pepper flakes; for a noticeably hot oil, use 5 tablespoons. If you can't decide, split the difference. Double or triple the recipe and it will happily wait for you in the fridge for months. Give some away. Squirrel the rest away for yourself. You'll put it on everything.

MAKES 1½ CUPS

1 cup peanut or safflower oil

3 to 5 tablespoons crushed red pepper flakes

1 tablespoon toasted sesame oil

2 tablespoons unsalted peanuts, minced

1 teaspoon salt

1 teaspoon sugar

In a small saucepan set over medium heat, combine the oil along with the crushed red pepper flakes.

Heat the oil to 300°F, then remove the pan from the heat and try not to breathe in the fumes! Let the oil cool to 250°F, then add the sesame oil and peanuts. Transfer to a clean glass jar. Add the salt and sugar. Seal the jar with a tight-fitting lid, shake it a few times to distribute the ingredients, and leave it at room temperature for 2 days. Shake it up whenever you think about it, a few times a day. After 2 days, move it to the refrigerator. It will keep for at least 1 month, if not longer, in the fridge.

Mushroom Larb *with Red and Green Cabbage and Spicy Lime Sauce*

Larb (or Laab) is typically a meat-based salad. It's one of the most exciting dishes in Thai cuisine, known for its burst of acidity, lively mix of herbs, and chile heat. In this version I use toasted millet and mushrooms to give the dish an earthy, satisfying base and feature cabbage both raw and cooked. The cabbage is sautéed until tender, and then it's used again raw as a "lettuce" cup.

SERVES 6

- 1 ounce dried shiitake mushroom caps (or ½-ounce sliced)
- ½ cup millet
- ¼ teaspoon salt
- 3½ ounces fresh maitake mushrooms
- ¼ cup high-heat oil, divided
- 1 pound green cabbage
- 1 pound red cabbage
- 2 tablespoons toasted rice powder (see Note)
- ½ red onion, halved, cored, and cut into ¼-inch half-moons
- 1 tablespoon liquid aminos (or fish sauce), plus more to taste
- 1 tablespoon gluten-free tamari (or soy sauce), plus more to taste
- ½ teaspoon crushed red pepper flakes, plus more to taste
- 2 minced Thai bird chiles (if you want it hot)
- 3 limes (2 juiced, 1 quartered for garnish), plus more lime juice to taste
- 1 teaspoon sugar
- 1 bunch mint leaves (about 1 loosely packed cup leaves)
- 1 bunch Thai basil (about 1 loosely packed cup leaves)
- ½ bunch cilantro, leaves and stems, roughly chopped
- ½ cup roasted peanuts
- Your favorite chile crisp, for topping the larb

Rehydrate the shiitake mushrooms in 2 cups of boiling water. Let the mushrooms sit in the water for 15 minutes, then strain the mushrooms, pressing on them to get all the liquid out, saving the liquid to use later. Mince up the caps.

Toast the millet in a medium saucepan until it starts to pop and turns light brown, 3 to 5 minutes. Add the shiitake rehydration liquid and the salt and bring to a boil. Reduce the heat to medium-low, cover, and cook for 18 minutes. Turn off the heat and leave covered for 10 more minutes, then fluff the millet.

Preheat a wok or saucepan over high heat. Trim the stem end of the maitake mushrooms; cut or tear the rest into bite-sized pieces. Add 2 tablespoons of the oil and, after a few moments, add the maitake mushrooms. Stir-fry until they start to brown, 3 to 4 minutes, then add the minced shiitake mushrooms and continue to cook until all the mushrooms are caramelized, about 3 to 4 more minutes. Turn down the

continues ➤

heat to medium. For both cabbages, cut into quarters, take the cores out, and mince them. Use the outside leaves as cups and cut the rest into ½-inch strips (refer to the photo on page 190 to see what the cups look like). Add the cabbage and stir-fry for 5 minutes, until it wilts. Add the remaining 2 tablespoons oil, then the steamed millet, and stir-fry together for a minute. Add the rice powder, onion, aminos, tamari, red pepper flakes, Thai bird chiles, lime juice, sugar, mint, Thai basil, cilantro, and peanuts. Toss it all together until the herbs soften, 1 to 2 minutes. Taste and add more aminos, tamari, lime juice, or red pepper flakes according to your taste.

Serve with the cabbage cups and garnish with chile crisp and a squeeze of lime.

Note

To make toasted rice powder, take ½ cup Thai sticky rice and toast in a medium skillet over medium to medium-low heat until the grains are golden brown—this takes patience and up to 20 minutes to achieve. You can't use sushi rice for this, but in a pinch jasmine rice will work. Once the rice is toasted, let cool for 10 minutes, then grind into a fine powder with a spice grinder or in a mortar and pestle. The good news: You can store it in a sealed container at room temperature for 2 months.

Homemade Kimchi *with Black Garlic*

Kimchi is arguably the most deeply delicious, funky, spicy, sour manifestation of the humble cabbage. The addition of black garlic gives this wildly loved and popular pickle an unusual, slightly caramel note. Kimchi can be refrigerated for up to a few months. Use clean utensils each time to grab some from the jar to keep it as fresh as possible. Korean red pepper flakes (gochugaru) are not as spicy as crushed red chile flakes and are powdered. If you love spicy food, use five tablespoons. If you want to keep it super mild, use one. I like a little heat and so I use three.

MAKE 2 CUPS

2 pounds Napa cabbage (about 1 medium)
¼ cup salt
Filtered (or distilled) water, as needed
2 black garlic cloves, sliced thin (or 1 tablespoon grated regular garlic)
1 tablespoon grated and peeled ginger
1 teaspoon sugar
2 tablespoons water
1 tablespoon liquid aminos (or fish sauce)
1 to 5 tablespoons gochugaru
1–2 pairs of disposable gloves

Using a large chef's knife or cleaver, cut the cabbage in half through the stem end. Using a "V" cut, cut along each side of the core and remove. Position the halves with the cut side down and cut crosswise into 1- to 2-inch strips. Find your biggest bowl and place the cut cabbage in it along with the salt.

Here's where you get super comfy with your food. Wash your hands well because you're going to give the cabbage a gentle yet firm Swedish massage, getting the salt worked into the cabbage. It will soften as you work with it. Spend about 2 to 3 min-

utes doing this. Next, cover the cabbage with water so the cabbage is just submerged. Place a plate directly on top of the submerged cabbage and find a large heavy can or similar item to weigh it down. Let it hang out at room temperature for 2 hours.

Meanwhile, in a small bowl, mix together the garlic, ginger, sugar, water, and liquid aminos. Stir in the gochugaru. Set aside.

After the cabbage has mingled with the salt water for 2 hours, it's time to rinse it a few times through a colander. Taste a piece. It should be well seasoned but not so salty you make a face. Let it drain in the colander for 10 minutes or so and then give it a squeeze to get rid of any extra moisture.

Don those gloves. In a large dry bowl, add the drained cabbage and, using a rubber spatula, get every last bit of chile mixture into the bowl with the cabbage and mix with your hands. The gloves are to keep the chiles from eventually getting in your eyes or on your sensitive skin. Once the chile mixture is worked into the cabbage (you don't need to be aggressive about this; just mix until it's well-coated), start packing the mixture into sterilized 1-quart jars (I recommend putting the jars and lids through the dishwasher or hand-washing and rinsing with boiling water to sterilize). With your gloved fist, press down on the cabbage so that the brine starts to come up and over the cabbage. This will prevent mold from forming on any exposed leaves. You want to have at least 1 inch of headspace at the top of the jar. Wipe up any spills, put the canning lid on top, and lightly turn the cap. Don't seal it tightly, as you don't want to build up too much pressure as the cabbage ferments.

Place the jars on a baking sheet or plate to catch any escaping brine, then leave at room temperature in a cool, non-sunny location anywhere from a few days to a week. Check on the kimchi once a day: open the lid and, using a clean spoon, push the cabbage back under the brine if any has surfaced. Taste each day and enjoy how it changes in flavor and starts to become acidic and a little funky in a good way. You may see bubbles. Enjoy them. It's a sign we are not alone in the universe. When it tastes good to you, transfer it to the fridge. In my experience, this is usually around day 5. Enjoy!

Escarole, Belgian and Frisée Endive

AKA
CICHORIUM ENDIVIA,
CURLY ENDIVE

AKA
CICHORIUM INTYBUS,
WITLOOF CHICORY

AKA
CICHORIUM ENDIVIA,
BROAD-LEAVED ENDIVE

THE 411: Escarole, Belgian endive, and frisée are all chicories, as is radicchio (see the Radicchio chapter on page 42). But I've separated them into two chapters because, while radicchio is at its best in midwinter to early spring, the rest of the chicories, generally speaking, are best in late fall, winter, and into early spring. When so little is growing in winter, it's worthwhile to understand our chicory friends.

ESCAROLE: Escarole is the mildest of all the chicories and can be used solo in salads as long as it's balanced with fatty ingredients or a rich dressing (see recipe on page 200).

BELGIAN ENDIVE: Wonderfully crisp, Belgian endive forms a natural cup just asking to be filled with deliciousness. Fantastic cut into strips or whole in salads, it's also lovely braised (see recipe on page 197).

FRISÉE: Frisée is light yellow and green, quite mild and delicate, and a welcome addition to other greens in a mixed salad. It holds up well in a warm salad of lentils or white beans.

AKA: Astute readers will notice that escarole and frisée are varieties of *endivia,* and Belgian endive is strangely in a different species, which is confusing! But luckily for cooks, as long as you can recognize the vegetable, it matters little what the taxonomic designation is. But for my fellow nerds out there, it's interesting to note how common names are clearly an inaccurate way to identify plants.

ESCAROLE: *Cichorium endivia,* broad-leaved endive

BELGIAN ENDIVE: *Cichorium intybus,* witloof chicory (Flemish for "white leaf" chicory)

FRISÉE: *Cichorium endivia,* curly endive

NUTRITION FACTS: Chicories are extremely nutritious. They are a rich source of inulin, a prebiotic that helps with digestive health. They are high in vitamins A and K, and are a good source of minerals and B-complex vitamins.

SEASON: Chicories, with the exception of radicchio, are best in late fall, winter, and into early spring.

PURCHASE, STORAGE, AND PREP TIPS: When purchasing chicories, look for vibrant leaves that show no signs of wilting or browning. If you are using Belgian endive for appetizers, get the larger ones so you will have more of the larger leaves for filling. Look for smaller heads of frisée, as the younger ones are a bit more tender with a fluffier texture that works well in salads. Store chicories in produce bags in your crisper drawer of the fridge. If they seem dry, wrap them loosely in a damp paper towel first. They will last for up to one week if stored properly. The cores of chicories tend to be quite bitter, so either cook or discard. For all chicory varieties, you can tone down any bitterness (if it doesn't suit your taste) by soaking cut leaves in cold water for 30 minutes.

ESCAROLE: The inner leaves of escarole are more mild than the tougher outer leaves. Use the inner leaves for salads and other raw preparations. The darker green outer leaves are better used in cooked dishes. For use in salads, cut in half lengthwise and make a "V" cut to remove the core, which can be discarded or cooked.

BELGIAN ENDIVE: To use endive for appetizers, trim the stem to release the leaves. You'll have to keep cutting bits off the stem as you work up the endive. Doing it gradually will preserve more of the leaf. For use in salads, cut in half lengthwise and make a "V" cut to remove the core, which can be discarded or cooked.

FRISÉE: Trim off the darker outer leaves and reserve for cooking. Use the inner light green and white leaves in salads. For use in salads, cut in half lengthwise and make a "V" cut to remove the core, which can be discarded or cooked. Because frisée can be very delicate, it's best to hand tear leaves for salads. Dress with vinaigrette right before serving so it doesn't wilt.

COOKING TIPS:

ESCAROLE: Escarole is lovely in soups and doesn't need much time to cook, 10 minutes max. It's also a great candidate for a high-heat, fast sauté. Add a little liquid to help it steam a bit, then evaporate that liquid.

BELGIAN ENDIVE: Unless it's cut into small pieces, Belgian endive takes time to get tender. I recommend (as in the Pan-Seared Endive recipe on page 197) to cut it in half lengthwise, brown the halves cut side down, and then cook with liquid.

FRISÉE: Frisée is best uncooked, but its outer leaves (which are tougher and more bitter than other varieties) are great added to soups and stews. The more tender leaves can be wilted under warm vinaigrettes, and they hold up well.

SUBS:

ESCAROLE: Swiss chard would be a good sub, as its leaves are similar. Mustard greens pack more of a bite, but cut with spinach or romaine would be a fair approximation.

BELGIAN ENDIVE: Napa cabbage has some of the crunch but not quite the same flavor, as it doesn't have that mild bitter edge. Frisée and arugula would give you some of that bite but obviously not the ability to use for appetizers.

FRISÉE: First look to arugula, another delicate, peppery green. Endive and radicchio cut into ribbons would give you a similar flavor profile.

Pan-Seared Endive *with Balsamic-Roasted Grapes, Feta, and Toasted Pumpkin Seeds*

This is a fairly straightforward and simple recipe that highlights how the bitterness in chicories can be such a lovely and interesting addition to recipes. If you're familiar with cocktails, you are already aware of how important bitters can be in balancing a drink. The same can be said for recipes. But everything must be in balance—which is why fat (feta) and sweetness (roasted grapes) have been added in this recipe. Have you ever tried roasted grapes? I remember the first time I did. I was like, why have I never thought of doing this before? They are pleasantly sweet and tart, concentrated down to a plum-fig jam-like depth. Combined with the warm feta? Stop it.

SERVES 4

2 tablespoons olive oil, plus a splash for the pumpkin seeds

1½ pounds Belgian endive, ends trimmed, cut in half lengthwise

1 teaspoon salt, divided, plus more to taste

¼ cup dry white vermouth or white wine

¾ pound red grapes, picked from stems

2 tablespoons balsamic vinegar

¼ cup pumpkin seeds

2 tablespoons toasted pumpkin oil (found in specialty markets or online; sub with good olive oil)

3 ounces sheep feta

Flaky salt, for garnish (optional)

Preheat the oven to 450°F. Line a baking sheet with parchment paper.

Add 2 tablespoons of olive oil to a large skillet and heat over medium-high heat. Add the endive cut side down, in two batches if necessary. Season with ½ teaspoon salt. Cook until deeply caramelized on the cut side, 5 to 7 minutes. Flip the endive over, add the vermouth, and cook for 4 to 5 minutes more, until a knife can be easily inserted. Set aside. Meanwhile, place the grapes on the baking sheet. Toss them with the balsamic vinegar and then season them with the other ½ teaspoon salt. Roast until they are blistery and their grapey goodness is all over the parchment paper. In a good way. (A bad way, in case that is your next question, is if they explode all over your oven and then you write me an email.) This should take 10 to 20 minutes or so. Once they come

continues ➡

out of the oven, pull the grapes with their parchment paper off the pan. You'll need to use this sheet pan again.

Toss the pumpkin seeds onto the baking sheet with a splash of olive oil and a pinch of salt. Mix up and toast them in the hot oven, watching them very carefully, until they puff and brown a bit, 4 to 5 minutes. (Alterna-tively, you can toast them in a skillet on the stove.) Set them aside for use as a garnish.

Plate the endive, cut side up. Scatter the grapes on and around the endive. Drizzle the pumpkin oil on everything, then scatter the feta over the top. Add a bit of flaky salt, if you'd like. Finally, and with great drama, let the pumpkin seeds fly.

Frisée and Quinoa Salad *with Tart Cherries and Maple-Citrus Dressing*

A lot of this hearty and satisfying grain salad can be made ahead. The maple-citrus dressing can be made up to a week ahead, and you'll have extra to use for other salads. The quinoa can be cooked up to two days before you need it, and the cherries can be pickled up to a week ahead. The sweet potatoes can be roasted a few days ahead as well. And while you're doing that, go ahead and toast the almonds. The day you make the salad, it's just a matter of tossing everything together. Or, if you have an hour to spare, make everything the same day you're serving it!

SERVES 4

FOR THE SALAD
¼ cup seasoned rice vinegar
½ cup dried tart cherries
2 cups water
1 cup red quinoa
2½ teaspoons salt, divided
1 pound sweet potatoes, unpeeled, medium diced
3 tablespoons olive oil
1 head curly frisée (6 ounces)
½ cup sliced almonds, toasted

FOR THE MAPLE-CITRUS DRESSING
Reserved rice vinegar from cherry pickling, plus ¼ cup more
¼ cup lemon juice
2 tablespoons maple syrup
2 teaspoons Dijon mustard
1 teaspoon salt
1 cup olive oil

TO MAKE THE SALAD

Preheat the oven to 450°F. Line a baking sheet with parchment paper.

In a small mason jar, add the seasoned rice vinegar and the cherries, put the lid on, shake it up, and let it sit while you wait for the quinoa and sweet potatoes to finish cooking.

In a small pot over high heat, bring the water to a boil. Add the quinoa and 1½ teaspoons of the salt, let it boil for 2 minutes, and then turn the heat down to a gentle simmer. Cover the pot and time it for 13 minutes. Keep the pot covered, pull it off the heat, and let it sit with the cover on for 10 minutes. No peeking! Fluff the quinoa and set it aside.

Place the sweet potato cubes on the baking sheet. Add the olive oil, mix well, and then season with the remaining 1 teaspoon salt. Roast in the oven for about 20 minutes, or until the sweet potatoes are lightly browned and tender.

Drain the cherries and save the liquid.

TO MAKE THE DRESSING

Combine all the dressing ingredients except the olive oil with an immersion blender or in a blender. On low speed, add the olive oil until it is all incorporated.

TO ASSEMBLE

Prep the frisée as explained on page 196, tearing it into small, bite-sized pieces. In a large bowl, add the quinoa, frisée, cherries, sweet potatoes, and almonds. Add half the dressing and gently mix the salad with a rubber spatula. Taste and add more dressing if you need it. Serve!

Escarole Salad *with Poached Egg, Roasted Tomatoes, and Pumpernickel Croutons*

Escarole has just the right texture—firm, hearty, almost like an edible succulent—that holds up brilliantly to the hearty ingredients in this salad. Feel free to substitute regular croutons if you can't find pumpernickel bread in your local store (look for it in a rectangular package in the bread section). The croutons can be made several days in advance. When cool, put them in an airtight container and leave at room temperature. You can poach the eggs up to 2 days before you need them. Simply transfer the poached eggs to a container with ice water and refrigerate. To reheat, carefully place them in simmering water for 1 minute. Then transfer to a towel to dry off before seasoning and serving. You can make the dressing days before you need it. You can double or quadruple the dressing recipe to have some on hand for salads during the rest of the week.

SERVES 4

FOR THE DRESSING

3 tablespoons apple cider vinegar
1 teaspoon Dijon mustard
1½ teaspoons honey
¼ cup olive oil
Salt, to taste
Freshly ground black pepper, to taste

FOR THE SALAD

6 ounces pumpernickel bread, small cubed
¼ cup plus 2 tablespoons olive oil, divided, plus more to taste
1¾ teaspoons salt, divided, plus more to taste
Freshly ground black pepper, as needed
1 pint cherry tomatoes, cut in half
2 teaspoons distilled vinegar (or white wine vinegar)
4 eggs
1 bunch escarole (10 to 12 ounces)
2 ounces Pecorino Romano, shaved
1 lemon, cut in half

Preheat the oven to 450°F. Line a baking sheet with parchment paper.

TO MAKE THE DRESSING

Add the vinegar, mustard, and honey to a small bowl and whisk. While whisking, slowly drizzle in the olive oil (or add everything to a mason jar and shake). Season to taste with salt and freshly ground black pepper.

TO MAKE THE CROUTONS AND ROAST THE TOMATOES

Add the pumpernickel cubes to the baking sheet and toss well with ¼ cup of the olive oil and ¼ teaspoon each of salt and pepper, to taste. Bake for 12 to 18 minutes, until crunchy. Slide the croutons off onto a plate and reuse the baking sheet and parchment paper for the cherry tomatoes. Add the tomatoes to the pan, along with ½ teaspoon salt. Roast for 20 to 25 minutes, until the tomatoes start to caramelize and have shriveled a bit.

TO POACH THE EGGS

Fill a large skillet (nonstick if you have it) nearly to the rim with water, add the remaining 1 teaspoon salt and the distilled vinegar, and bring the mixture to a boil over high heat. Crack the eggs into individual small-handled cups or ramekins. Lower the lips of each cup into the water as carefully and quickly as you can, cover the pan, and remove from the heat. Time the eggs for 5 minutes for runny yolks and barely set whites, 6 minutes for just runny yolks and set whites, and 7 minutes for firmer yolks. With a slotted spoon, carefully lift and drain each egg over the skillet and then onto a towel. Season to taste with salt and pepper and serve immediately.

TO ASSEMBLE

Prep the escarole as explained on page 196. Cut into bite-sized pieces. Add to a large bowl along with the pumpernickel croutons. Add the dressing and mix well with your hands. Plate the salad in four shallow bowls. Top each salad with an equal portion of the cherry tomatoes, a poached egg, and the shaved cheese. Squeeze some lemon over the salads and serve.

Fennel

AKA
FOENICULUM VULGARE,
FLORENCE FENNEL,
FINOCCHIO

THE 411: You gotta love a venerated and prized vegetable: In ancient Greek mythology, Prometheus used a giant stalk of fennel to carry fire from Mount Olympus to humanity on Earth. The Greeks and Romans used it for medicine, food, and insect repellent. Health remedy, dinner, and bugs begone . . . all in one food. What a vegetable!

Indigenous to the Mediterranean but found widely throughout the world, fennel is one of the most versatile vegetables to add to your repertoire, as every part, save the roots, is edible. Fennel bulbs and stems can be eaten raw or cooked, and the fronds are a fantastic addition to salads and dips, or as garnishes. The bright yellow fennel pollen can be used in rubs or sprinkled over salads and cheeses. The seeds, when fresh and green or when fully dried and gray-brown, are used in many spice blends, on their own in cooking, or in teas and for flavoring liquors.

India is the top producer of fennel, followed by China (but this may be a bit misleading, as production data from the UN Food and Agriculture Organization groups anise, star anise, and coriander in with fennel). In the United States you'll see wild fennel along highways, coastlines, and especially in places with Mediterranean-like sea breezes. This wild fennel grows much taller than the Florence fennel, which is cultivated for its large, sweet bulb. Wild fennel can be quite invasive. In fact, Santa Cruz Island in California is nearly buried in it, and the plant has choked out many native species. While you can harvest the seeds and fronds of wild fennel, there is no real bulb to speak of.

Along with winter citrus, fennel brings this lovely, bright, light, sunshine-y flavor into the kitchen, especially in climates where the winter days are short and the sun is absent (as I write this from gray, drizzly Seattle). So why is it misunderstood? There is confusion between bulb fennel and wild fennel, and the common mislabeling of fennel as "anise" (it's not, and anise seed comes from the anise plant, not fennel). As a result, people who don't understand fennel tend to equate it with black licorice, and if they don't like black licorice, they don't buy or eat fennel. Here's the skinny: while it's true that the compound anethole is present in both licorice and fennel and gives it its familiar (if detested by some) flavor, fennel has much less of this compound and it's most present in the raw form. Once cooked, especially braised until yielding and buttery, the licorice flavor is nearly gone. Sworn licorice haters in my purely anecdotal experience have loved it. Hate black licorice or are you cooking for someone who does? Try the recipe for Juniper-Braised Fennel with Green Olives and Shallots (page 207) and see if that changes minds.

AKA: *Foeniculum vulgare,* Florence fennel, *finocchio* (Italian). Often incorrectly misidentified as "anise."

NUTRITION FACTS: Fennel is high in iron, vitamins A and C, and calcium. It is commonly used around the world as a digestive. Research has shown that it aids digestion by reducing inflammation in the bowels. In India, the seeds are candied and eaten after meals.

SEASON: A cool-weather crop, fennel's prime season is winter. You'll start to see it come through the markets in mid-fall, and it will be available into the spring.

PURCHASE, STORAGE, AND PREP TIPS: Look for bulbs with the fronds still attached, as fresh fronds point to a recent harvest. The bulb should be dense, with no or very little browning on the outer stems. Avoid very large bulbs, as they tend to get stringy, tough, and hollow in the centers with age. Store fennel in produce bags in your crisper drawer. If you need to keep the fronds beyond a day or two, cut off the fronds, wrap in a dry paper towel, and place in their own bag. The fronds will last for 3 to 5 days. The bulbs can last for a few weeks if properly stored. To prep, simply slice a thin bit off the stem end and, using the knife blade, whittle off any bits on the outermost stalk that don't look perfect. You don't need to sacrifice the whole outer stem because of a spot here or there. Cut off the stems where they meet the bulb and use those for stock or as a celery substitute. If I cut fennel on a mandoline, I tend to cut it in half lengthwise and then put the halves, crosswise, through the blade on the thinnest setting.

COOKING TIPS: Roasting at high temperatures will sweeten up fennel bulb and bring out its best. Braising it (or sous-viding it) yields a super mellow version, great for folks who object to the licorice flavor. Fennel wedges can get a bit tough if cooked solely with dry heat, so I prefer to braise wedges with liquid to keep them tender. For roasting, I like to cut across the grain to help tenderize it.

SUBS: Celery stalks can sub for fennel stalks and vice versa. Onions and leeks (when cooked) carry the same sweet, savory note albeit without the subtle anise flavor. Bok choy stems or endive paired with ground fennel seed can cook up to a fairly decent proximity of fennel bulb. Caraway, dill, and anise seed can sub for fennel seeds.

Juniper-Braised Fennel
with Green Olives and Shallots

A dirty martini was the inspiration behind this dish. Instead of wine, why not a splash of gin? Juniper is in gin, so let's bump that up with some cracked juniper berries, which pair nicely with the herbal, anise flavor of the fennel. Oh, but I do like that olive brine in my martinis sometimes, so let's add that to the braising liquid for salt and that rich olive base note. Make sure to slightly crack the juniper berries so that you can easily retrieve them later—wrapping them in cheesecloth makes for easy retrieval. For a complete vegetarian meal, pair this with garlicky white beans, oven-dried tomatoes, and some sautéed greens.

SERVES 4

3 pounds fennel, with fronds (if possible)
¼ cup olive oil, divided
2 ounces shallot (1 medium), quartered
2 cracked juniper berries
¼ cup gin
½ cup water
4 tablespoons olive brine from the jar
¾ cup pitted Castelvetrano green olives
4 tablespoons unsalted butter, cut into small pieces
1 teaspoon sherry vinegar
1 mandarin orange, peeled, fruit cut into ¼-inch slices, for garnish

Preheat the oven to 350°F.

Cut the fennel where the stems meet the bulb. Pick off any fronds in small pieces and reserve for garnish. Reserve the stems for another use (see the box on page 210 for ideas on how to use them). Very lightly trim the stem end so the wedges will stay together. Cut the fennel into 1-inch wedges, measured at the fatter end.

Heat up a cast-iron skillet or other oven-safe skillet over medium-high heat. Add 2 tablespoons of the olive oil and sear half of the fennel slices, browning both cut sides well, about 5 to 7 minutes total cooking time. Remove to a plate while you heat up the rest of the olive oil and sear the rest of the fennel. Add the shallots in with the second batch of fennel to brown them as well. Remove the second batch of fennel and shallots to the plate.

Turn off the heat and let the pan cool for a few minutes. Nestle the fennel and shallots back into the pan along with the juniper berries (wrapped in cheesecloth, if you have some). Pour the gin, water, and olive brine over the top. Tuck the olives in and around the fennel. Top with the butter pieces and pop into the oven, uncovered, to braise for 30 minutes, or until the fennel is tender throughout. Stir in the sherry vinegar and remove the juniper berries. Garnish with the mandarin orange slices and reserved fennel fronds.

Fennel and Citrus Salad *with Feta and Mint*

Fennel and citrus are a marriage nearly as perfect as chocolate and peanut butter, but with a much smaller marketing budget. This is a simple winter weeknight salad where you lay everything out on a platter and then drizzle the oil over the top and liberally sprinkle on the herb and spice garnishes. Feel free to make it even simpler by cutting all the citrus into wheels or large cubes—no need to get fancy with the supreming technique (go to beckyselengut.com for a video tutorial on supreming citrus). If Meyer lemons are not available, just leave them out. I prefer French or Israeli sheep feta because it's creamier and less salty than the Greek feta available in most US supermarkets. The feta can therefore take a gentle backseat in the dish, allowing the fennel flavor to shine through.

SERVES 4

1 grapefruit (Rio Red, if available)

1 Meyer lemon

1 orange, peeled, cut in ¼-inch rounds

1 teaspoon salt, divided

¾ pound fennel bulb, with fronds (if possible), for garnish

½ cup Castelvetrano olives

½ cup sheep feta, crumbled

¼ cup olive oil

1 tablespoon pink peppercorns, lightly crushed (optional)

¼ cup mint, chopped, for garnish

Flaky sea salt, to taste

Grab two medium bowls. Over one, supreme the grapefruit and Meyer lemon. Squeeze out any extra juice from the rind into the bowl. Cut the oranges and lemons into rounds and place them in the bowl. Sprinkle ½ teaspoon of the salt over the citrus and gently mix. Tip out all the juice from the cit-rus bowl into the other bowl, where you will store the fennel to prevent it from oxidizing.

Cut the fennel where the stems meet the bulb. Pick off any fronds into small pieces and reserve for garnish. Reserve the stems (see the box on page 210 for ideas on how to use them). Cut the bulb in half lengthwise. Shave the fennel paper thin, using a mando-line to cut it across the grain over the bowl with the citrus juice. Season with the other ½ teaspoon of salt. Drain the fennel before plating.

On a platter or individual plates, place the fennel down first. Garnish with several sec-tions of each kind of citrus. Top with olives and feta. Drizzle the olive oil over the top and then garnish with the pink peppercorns. Scatter some mint and fennel fronds on the salad. Sprinkle a little flaky salt on top, to your taste, and serve right away.

Fennel Stems

What are they good for anyway?

1. **Save them for stock:** Add them to a freezer bag with thyme, parsley stems, onion skins, carrot tops, celery, mushroom stems, and the like. Keep the bag in the freezer and keep filling it up. When the bag is full, simply dump the large vegetable ice cube into a pot of water. Bring to a boil, simmer for 45 minutes, strain, and you have a quick and easy vegetable stock.

2. **Cook them:** While they tend to be hollow, they still have a nice, celery-like flavor. Cut them into rounds and sauté them in place of (or in addition to) celery and onion in your next soup or stew.

3. **Candy them:** Admittedly this is a cheffy fancy thing, but you can cut them into thin rounds, cook them in a simple syrup, lay them out on a piece of wax paper, and allow them to dry overnight. They make an unusual garnish for desserts.

4. **Jam them:** Fennel stems are super tasty when added to marmalades and jams, giving them that lovely mildly sweet anise flavor. My friend Abby makes her signature fennel marmalade with the stems.

5. **Cook on them:** Lay them crosswise over grill grates and cook on top of them. If you eat fish, give it a try. Or you can use them as a bed to protect smaller items from falling through the grates (simply skewer the stems together with metal skewers and place crosswise over grill grates). They will impart a lovely flavor to whatever you lay on top of them to cook. You want to get super fancy? Skewer in some rosemary branches between the fennel stems.

Caramelized Fennel, Potato, and Thyme Frittata

The fennel becomes meltingly tender in this recipe and has a particular affinity to the herbs and cream. All elements here work in concert to elevate your basic egg bake. The secret to good frittatas is a combination of low and slow cooking, and quick and hot cooking. Take the time to cook the vegetables separately, as this releases their moisture so the frittata doesn't become waterlogged. Plus, you must not fear fat. Fat is important. Fat is delicious. In this recipe, we par-cook the eggs on the stovetop, making sure they don't overcook on the bottom. Then we cook them hot and fast under the broiler so they puff up. Using a thermometer guarantees you don't overcook them, so make sure you have a digital one to get an accurate read.

SERVES 4

- 1½ pounds fennel with stems and fronds, if possible
- ½ red onion, cut into ¼-inch half-moons
- ½ pound fingerling potatoes, cut into ¼-inch rounds
- 3 tablespoons olive oil, plus a splash for topping
- 2 teaspoons salt, divided, more as needed
- Freshly ground black pepper
- 10 branches of thyme
- 12 eggs
- ¾ cup cream
- 2 ounces cream cheese
- 4 ounces goat cheese, divided
- 1 tablespoon white wine vinegar (optional)
- 2 tablespoons unsalted butter
- 1 cup cherry tomatoes, cut in half

Preheat the oven to 400°F. Line a baking sheet with parchment paper.

Cut the fennel where the stems meet the bulb. Pick off any fronds into small pieces and reserve for garnish. Reserve the stems for an optional garnish. Quarter the fennel bulb and cut crosswise into ¼-inch slices. Lovingly chuck the sliced fennel, onion, and potatoes onto the baking sheet. Toss with the olive oil. Mix well and spread everything out so that the vegetables can get caramelized. Sprinkle 1 teaspoon of the salt over the top. Add black pepper if you're into it. I'm into it. Take 8 of those thyme branches (reserve the rest and mince the leaves for an optional garnish) and tuck them under the veg, scattered about so they don't burn but perfume everything as it roasts. Pop the pan in the oven and cook until everything is tender and lightly browned and your house smells divine, about 30 minutes.

continues ➤

In a blender, combine the eggs, cream, cream cheese, and 2 ounces of the goat cheese (reserve the rest for later) into a smooth mixture.

For the optional garnish, thinly slice a few of the fennel stems and mix with about ½ cup of fronds or whatever you have. Add a pinch of salt, a splash of olive oil, the white wine vinegar, and the chopped thyme. Taste for seasoning. It should be herbal and acidic to contrast with the rich frittata. Set aside.

Turn on your broiler and put a rack in the middle. Season the egg mixture with the other teaspoon of salt, mixing it up with a whisk. Heat a 10- to 12-inch nonstick oven-safe skillet or a well-seasoned cast-iron pan over medium heat. Add the butter, swirl it around, and add the vegetables. Turn down the heat to low and add the eggs. If you are using cast iron, wait at least 2 minutes to allow the pan to cool off a bit so you don't overcook the eggs. Using a rubber spatula, gently pull the eggs from the outside toward the middle so that the eggs flow behind your spatula. Do this until the eggs start to feel set on the bottom, a couple of minutes.

Scatter the tomato pieces and the rest of the goat cheese over the top of the frittata. Place the pan in the oven to finish cooking. Watch carefully; it should only take 3 to 5 minutes to finish cooking the eggs. Lean on undercooking them a bit, as they will continue to cook off the heat. Use a thermometer to determine doneness. You are looking for 160°F.

Take the frittata out of the oven and let the frittata sit for a bit before attempting an unmolding. Carefully tip the frittata out of the pan onto a platter and cut into wedges. Or serve it in the pan, especially if you are using cast iron. Look on page 212 and you'll see I served it right from the pan! Garnish the top with the optional fennel-thyme garnish.

Mustard Greens

AKA
BRASSICA JUNCEA, CURLY
OR CURLED MUSTARD,
MUSTARD SPINACH, INDIAN
MUSTARD, LEAF MUSTARD

THE 411: Kale is so yesterday (I joke, kale is yesterday, today, and tomorrow). Make room for mustard greens: a more robust, slightly peppery green that brings a horseradish-like note to your dishes. There are many varieties of mustard green (leaf mustard, Korean red mustard, Japanese giant red mustard, snow mustard, and curled leaf mustard). In my experience, while they may look slightly different and have subtle differences in flavor, all the varieties can be integrated into your cooking in the same way. The leaves can be added in small pieces to salads to boost flavor and nutritional value; added to green smoothies, soups, and stews; and used for pickling. Mustard greens are highly regarded in many cuisines of the world, but they are especially celebrated in Nepali, Indian, Chinese, and Japanese cuisine. They are an important part of soul food in Black cooking traditions of the US South.

Mustard, the plant, has been cultivated across Asia and Europe for centuries and is thought to have originated in the Himalayan region of India over 5,000 years ago. The edible seeds of the mustard plant are ground to make mustard and pressed to make oil. Mustard seeds have been found in ancient Greek archaeological sites. In medieval Europe you could be employed as a "mustardarius," and your job would be to manage the growing and production of mustard. Botanists have linked the Sichuan area of China to the major secondary sources of genetic variation to the mustard plant.

Do you enjoy arugula? The pepperiness we associate with arugula is similar to the horseradish-like sharpness of mustard greens. There is a slight bitterness that comes along for the ride in mustard greens, not unlike other members of the cruciferous family. Adding acidic ingredients, such as citrus juice and vinegar, plus cooking them in fat helps to balance out their sharp, slightly bitter and spicy flavor. Younger, smaller mustard greens are a bit more mild than older, larger greens.

AKA: *Brassica juncea,* curly or curled mustard, mustard spinach, Indian mustard, leaf mustard.

NUTRITION FACTS: Mustard greens are high in vitamins A, C, and K (very high in K), and a moderate source of calcium and vitamin E.

SEASON: A cool-weather crop, mustard greens are happy in the winter and really shine when not much else is going on in the garden. That being said, you can find them from fall through spring in markets.

PURCHASE, STORAGE, AND PREP TIPS: As with all greens, look for robust leaves that look full of life and are not limp, shriveled, or bug eaten. Store mustard greens wrapped, unwashed (to avoid moisture-related mold issues), in a dry paper towel in a produce bag in the crisper drawer of your fridge. To prep mustard greens, you can keep the stems attached or you can separate stems from leaves to give the stems a little head start in cooking. It's up to you. Sometimes I like the combination of more texture in the stems and meltingly tender leaves. For other preparations, I cook them separately.

COOKING TIPS: If you want to tame some of the spiciness of mustard greens, a quick blanch and shock (boil in salted water and chill in ice water) will make them more mild. You can then proceed to sauté them with aromatics.

SUBS: Turnip, radish, kohlrabi, or beet greens are a great substitute and have some of the peppery bite of mustard greens. Kale, spinach, collard greens, or chard would also work in a pinch.

Mustard Greens Saag Paneer

Saag paneer (leafy greens with paneer cheese) is one of my favorite Indian recipes. When it's made with just spinach, it's called palak paneer. But you can use any leafy green or a mix to make this dish. I like a mix of spinach and mustard greens, but save up your beet and turnip greens to add to this dish as well. Serve this over basmati rice with plenty of mango chutney on the side, as it is a great balance to the slightly bitter mustard greens.

SERVES 4

¼ teaspoon turmeric

⅛ teaspoon freshly ground black pepper

3 tablespoons garam masala

1 teaspoon plus ¼ teaspoon salt, divided, more as needed

8 ounces paneer, cubed

2 tablespoons ghee, divided, or 1 tablespoon butter plus 1 tablespoon high-heat oil

1 pound mustard greens, stems separated from leaves

1 onion, small diced

1 jalapeño, seeds and membranes removed (or left in if you like it spicier), minced

2 tablespoons grated ginger

1 pound spinach

1 cup water

1 cup cream

1 tablespoon honey

1 lemon, juiced

1 tablespoon kasuri methi (dried fenugreek leaves; optional)

Cooked basmati rice, for serving

Mango chutney, for serving

Heat a large well-seasoned cast-iron or non-stick sauté pan over medium-high heat.

In a small bowl, whisk together the turmeric, black pepper, garam masala, and ¼ teaspoon salt. In a medium bowl, take one-half of the spice mix and combine with the paneer cubes. Turn down the heat to medium. Add 1 tablespoon of the ghee to the sauté pan and then add the paneer cubes and sear them on one side (to keep them from drying out) until they brown, about 2 to 3 minutes. Remove to a plate.

Chop the mustard stems into small dice. Reheat the pan over medium-high heat, add the other tablespoon of ghee to the pan and then the onion, jalapeño, and 1 teaspoon of salt. Sauté until the onions start to soften and begin to brown, about 10 minutes. Add the rest of the spice mix and stir for a minute, until you can smell the spices. Add the mustard stems and ginger and cook for another 5 minutes. Add the mustard green leaves, spinach (with stems), water, cream, honey, lemon juice, and optional kasuri methi. Simmer the greens for 10 more minutes, until they are nice and tender. Season to taste. Using an immersion blender or regular blender, blend to a chunky consistency (or smooth, if you prefer). Place the mixture back in the skillet over medium heat, and add the paneer. When the paneer is warmed through, serve with basmati rice and mango chutney.

Mustard Greens and Spinach
with Toasted Sesame Dressing

This dish is based on the Japanese dish goma-ae, *which is traditionally made with just spinach. The addition of the mustard greens adds a depth of flavor, a very slight bitterness, and a punch of peppery heat. You can toast the sesame seeds in a dry pan over medium-high heat. Keep an eye on them so they don't burn. Don't skip this step, as it's an important part of the flavor in this dish.*

SERVES 4

1 tablespoon salt, plus more as needed

1 bunch mustard greens

½ pound spinach

¼ cup sesame seeds, lightly toasted

1 tablespoon sugar

2 tablespoons gluten-free tamari
(or soy sauce)

1 teaspoon mirin

1 teaspoon sake

1 teaspoon toasted sesame oil, plus more
as needed

1 teaspoon seasoned rice vinegar, plus more
as needed

Fill a large pot with water and bring to a boil, then add the salt to the pot. While the water is boiling, prepare an ice bath in a large bowl.

Separate the mustard greens from the stems. Save the stems for another use. Trim just the very bottom of the spinach stems off, but keep the majority of the stems attached (they are tender and delicious in this dish). Boil (blanch) the mustard greens for 1 minute. Leave them in the pot and then add the spinach and boil for 1 more minute. Remove or strain out both greens and immediately shock them in ice water. Drain the greens and squeeze out as much water as you can. Lay the greens onto a cutting board and slice them into 1-inch sections, then set them aside.

In either a mortar and pestle or in a spice grinder, grind the sesame seeds and sugar to medium fine (just a couple of pulses in an electric grinder). Remove the sugar-sesame mixture from the mortar and pestle; combine it with the tamari, mirin, sake, sesame oil, and rice vinegar; and mix well into the drained greens. Have a bite and add more salt, sesame oil, or rice vinegar to your taste. Serve.

Pasta *with Mustard Cream and Sun-Dried Tomatoes*

Sun-dried tomatoes are an incredible ingredient that hit the US like a storm in the '80s, but then they fell by the wayside for reasons I don't understand. They are an umami-packed powerhouse that deliver an incredible richness to anything they touch. The mustard greens bring the pepper to this pasta dish, and the mushrooms contribute more umami and earthiness. Feel free to use any shape of tubular dried pasta you have on hand for this (penne, ziti, rigatoni). The mustard cream tucks inside the hollows of the pasta, flavoring it from both the inside and out.

SERVES 4

2 tablespoons plus 1 teaspoon salt, divided

2 tablespoons unsalted butter

1 red onion, thinly sliced, divided

½ cup dry white wine or dry white vermouth

1 bunch mustard greens, stems removed and reserved for another use

1½ cups cream

½ cup vegetable stock

1 bay leaf

A few sprigs of hearty herbs like thyme, rosemary, or sage

1 cup roughly chopped parsley

1 teaspoon white wine vinegar, more as needed

8 ounces mushrooms, such as maitake or king trumpet

2 tablespoons olive oil

1 pound penne pasta (or any tubular pasta you like)

One 7-ounce jar of sun-dried tomatoes, drained and sliced into bite-sized pieces

Preheat the oven to 400°F. Line a baking sheet with parchment paper. Bring a large pot of water with 2 tablespoons of salt in it to a boil.

Heat a large skillet with straight sides over medium-high heat. Add the butter and, when melted, add half of the onions along with ½ teaspoon of the salt. Cook, stirring from time to time, until the onions start to brown a bit, around 15 minutes. Deglaze the pan with the white wine and simmer until the wine has evaporated off. Add the mustard greens (save 2 mustard leaves and chiffonade them into very tiny ribbons for garnish, see the photo on page 221) and sauté until they start to soften, about 5 minutes. Turn down the heat to medium-low, add the cream and stock along with the bay leaf and hearty herb sprigs and simmer until slightly thickened, about 10 minutes. Remove the herb stems and discard. Transfer the onion-cream mixture to a blender, along with the parsley and vinegar. Puree until smooth.

Rinse out the skillet, put it back on the stove, and add the puree to it. Let it sit off the heat.

Chop the mushrooms into bite-sized pieces and place on the baking sheet along with the rest of the onion. Add the olive oil and another ½ teaspoon of the salt, mix well, spread out, and roast for about 20 minutes, until the mushrooms and onions are caramelized.

Add the pasta to the boiling water and cook until al dente. While the pasta is cook-ing, reheat the sauce on low heat. Drain the pasta and save 1 cup of pasta cooking water.

Add the pasta to the skillet and stir it into the sauce. Add the mushroom-onion mix-ture. Add most of the sun-dried tomatoes (save some for garnish). Taste the pasta. If it needs more salt, stir in some of the pasta cooking water (which is salty). Add more vin-egar if it needs a bit of brightness. Plate the pasta and garnish with a few sun-dried toma-toes and the chiffonade of mustard greens.

Jicama

AKA
PACHYRHIZUS EROSUS, MEXICAN POTATO, MEXICAN TURNIP, CHINESE POTATO, SWEET TURNIP, YAM BEAN

THE 411: Jicama is—here we go again—not a vegetable at all but a legume. The part we eat is the tuber. All other parts of the vine are poisonous. Native to Mexico and Central America, it is also widely eaten in Asia. It's mostly eaten for its refreshingly crisp and juicy texture, as the flavor is somewhat subtle. Think apple or Asian pear, but not as sweet. It's reminiscent of water chestnut but less dense.

There are two varieties of jicama found in Mexico: *jicama de agua,* which is the one we see in our marketplaces, and *jicama de leche,* which has an elongated root and is named for the milky color of its juices. *Jicama de leche* is a little less sweet than *jicama de agua.*

Why Is Jicama Misunderstood by Some Folks?

1. It doesn't have a come-hither beautiful exterior, which causes many to walk right by it.
2. Non-Spanish speakers fear pronouncing it incorrectly. It's not ja-CAME-uh, but HEE-ka-ma.
3. It tastes like a fruit, can be cooked like a vegetable, but is technically a legume.

AKA: *Pachyrhizus erosus,* Mexican potato, Mexican turnip, Chinese potato, sweet turnip, yam bean.

NUTRITION FACTS: Jicama is 90 percent water, which basically means it's a food and a drink. It's high in vitamin C and fiber, and that's about it folks. Oh, wait, there's more: it's also high in what's known as a prebiotic, an indigestible sugar called inulin (see also: Sunchokes, page 170), which is great for your gut biome and maybe not so great for your social life. So eaters should use the same caution with jicama as they might use when contemplating eating a huge bowl of Brussels sprouts.

SEASON: Jicama is at its best in the winter, though in the United States you will start seeing it (imported from Mexico) from October through May.

PURCHASE, STORAGE, AND PREP TIPS: You want to look for a medium-sized tuber (about the size of a large grapefruit), as they can get fibrous when large. They can grow to be up to 50 pounds! That's a fun fact, but don't buy that one. It should look and feel heavy for its size. Squeeze it to make sure it's firm, and give it a smell to make sure there are no off odors. Make sure it's not wrinkled or shriveled at all and that there is no mold. The skin should be smooth and dry, and preferably thin. If it has a slight silky sheen, all the better. Jicamas can go off if they have experienced extreme variations in temperature, they're old, or in transit they were used as a soccer ball. Annoyingly, they can go brown on the inside but still look OK on the outside. Jicama that is brown throughout on the inside is not good. A little spot of brown here or there can be cut out, but toss tubers that are discolored throughout. Just between us, if you want to be sure you're getting a good one, give it a little nick with your nail to check for juiciness and get a look-see that the inside is bright white and not brown. Do this on the down-low. Destroy this book now. If that makes you nervous, ask the produce person to cut your jicama in half to make sure it's a good one, then buy it.

To store jicama, keep it dry! It can stay fresh for months if it's kept whole, dry, and stored between 55° and 59°F. For short-term storage (up to three weeks), keep it in a cool, dark location (no bag necessary). You could also store it in the fridge, wrapped in a paper towel, to make sure it stays dry. Once you cut into it, you'll need to keep it in a produce bag or sealed container and use it up within a few days to one week. To prep jicama, wash it well and dry it. Then cut off both ends and use a knife or peeler to remove the skin. The flesh does not oxidize rapidly, so you do not need to store it in acidulated water or rub it with a lemon.

COOKING TIPS: While many prefer to eat jicama raw (to best appreciate its refreshing texture), it holds up well to cooking, keeping some of its texture. If you know you can't get through a whole jicama raw and you happen to be roasting vegetables, throw some on the pan or cook some cubes in a soup.

SUBS: Sunchokes are a good substitute for jicama, as they provide a similar texture (but are less juicy). Water chestnuts can be used in a pinch, and daikon radish both looks and crunches just like jicama but will give you more of a peppery, radish vibe.

Jicama "Elotes"

Elote means "corn cob" in Spanish, and the word is used to describe Mexican street corn where the corn is grilled and then smeared in a cheesy-mayo-chile mixture. I've taken the flavors of elotes and combined them with sticks of jicama to make an appetizer that delivers a similar sweetness with the added value of the crunchiness of the jicama. Serve these as appetizers before a dinner of quesadillas, tostadas, or chile relleno. (You can tuck squash blossoms into your quesadillas to enjoy a traditional Mexican dish.) This recipe can also easily be used to make esquites, which is elotes off the cob. Simply dice the jicama into cubes, add some charred corn (cut off the cob), and combine with the other ingredients listed.

SERVES 4 TO 8

2 pounds jicama, peeled

2 limes, zested and juiced

¼ cup mayonnaise

¼ cup finely chopped cilantro

⅛ teaspoon cayenne pepper

½ teaspoon ancho chile pepper

4 ounces cotija cheese, crumbled into tiny pieces

1 tablespoon Tajín (see Note), for garnish

Cut the jicama into *batonnet* (French for "small sticks"—technically, ¼ inch by ¼ inch by 2 to 2½ inches). Place a small skewer or sturdy appetizer toothpick into the end of each jicama stick.

In a small bowl, combine the lime zest, lime juice, mayonnaise, cilantro, cayenne pepper, ancho chile pepper, and half of the cotija cheese. Holding the jicama by the skewer or appetizer toothpick, roll the jicama sticks through the lime-mayo or spoon it onto the jicama. Make sure to leave the end closest to the toothpick free of sauce to show off the white of the jicama in contrast to the coated part. Place on a platter, sprinkle some Tajín on each piece, and sprinkle the rest of the cotija on top.

Note

Tajín (pronounced ta-heen) is a popular Mexican chile seasoning that's made from chiles, dehydrated lime, and salt. You can find it in the Mexican section of supermarkets. It is incredible when sprinkled on mango.

Jicama Aguachile

Aguachile ("chile water" in Spanish) is a vibrant, spicy Mexican dish made by soaking shrimp in a mixture of lime juice, chiles, and herbs. It has many variations, but you'll typically find onions, cucumbers, and avocado in the mix. On a trip to Zihuatanejo to relax and hang out with our friends Pedro and Yieri (and their family), they introduced us to Chef Jorge Murillo and Ariana Avila at their restaurant, Sr. Aguachile. There, we had a vegetarian version of one of the best aguachiles I've ever had, which featured jicama instead of shrimp. The jicama was shaved paper thin and formed the base of the dish. Inspired, I developed my own version of it, using hearts of palm, which give the dish a meaty texture, similar to crab. This is hot-weather, ice-cold cerveza food to eat with a pile of salty totopos (tortilla chips). If you find yourself in Zihua, as the locals call it, check out our friend Pedro's tour company, Zihua Tours, and stop in for a meal at Sr. Aguachile.

SERVES 4

¼ red onion, cut into thin half-moons

1 tablespoon red wine vinegar

½ teaspoon salt, plus more to taste

½ bunch cilantro (stems, too!)

½ bunch parsley (stems, too!)

1 jalapeño (2 if you like it spicy)

½ cup freshly squeezed lime juice (3 to 4 limes)

½ cup freshly squeezed orange juice (1 orange)

1 pound jicama, peeled

1 small Persian cucumber, sliced thin (or ½ regular cucumber, peeled and seeded)

One 14-ounce can hearts of palm, drained and shredded

1 avocado, sliced

Flaky salt, as needed

2 tablespoons olive oil

Tortilla chips, as needed

Pickle the red onions with the red wine vinegar and a pinch of salt as instructed on page 115.

Add the cilantro, parsley, jalapeño, ½ teaspoon salt, and citrus juices to a blender jar and blend until bright green and smooth. Taste and adjust the seasoning. You want a very bright, spicy, and herbal mixture. Pour the mixture into a large bowl and set aside.

Dice the jicama and/or cut into thin ribbons with a mandoline. Add the jicama, cucumber, and hearts of palm to the bowl with the green sauce. Toss gently and plate. Pour extra sauce around the plate or platter. Top with avocado slices. Garnish with flaky salt. Drizzle the olive oil over the top.

Serve the aguachile with tortilla chips.

Rice Paper Rolls *with Jicama,*
Fresh Herbs, and Mango

Fact: this is one of the fussier recipes in this book. It takes practice to learn how to work with the rice paper wrappers if you're new to it. There is only one way to get better at making these, and that's by making a lot of them. The end result is worth it! Prep as much as you can a day ahead: the cashews can be toasted, the mango and jicama can be cut and stored in the fridge, and the sauce can be made. On the day of, you can prepare the noodles, lay everything out, and start rolling. These rolls are best eaten within a few hours, and I highly recommend, if you are not serving them right away, to individually wrap them in plastic wrap. You can leave them out at room temperature for four hours safely, and they are best when they haven't seen the inside of a refrigerator.

SERVES 4

4 ounces rice vermicelli noodles

1 head butter lettuce

½ cup green mango, cut into thin
  matchsticks

½ cup ripe mango, cut into thin matchsticks

½ cup jicama, cut into thin matchsticks

½ cup cashews, toasted

¼ cup Thai basil, roughly chopped

¼ cup mint, leaves picked off stems

1 package edible flowers (optional)

1 package rice paper wrappers, 8½ inches
  wide (look for the Three Ladies brand)

Black garlic chile sauce (recipe follows)
  or purchased sweet Thai chile sauce

Soak the noodles in warm water to cover for 20 minutes. Meanwhile, bring enough water to cover noodles up to a boil in a pot or kettle. After the soak, drain the noodles, place back in a bowl, and pour the boiling water over the noodles. Test them for tenderness after a few minutes. They should be cooked through but still have a bit of a bite to them. It should take 3 to 5 minutes. Drain the noodles in a colander and pour cold water over them to stop the cooking process.

If you want to make the rolls as pictured on page 229, you'll be layering the ingredients one by one into the wrappers (first put down one lettuce leaf, then some noodles, then tuck in both types of mango pieces, jicama, cashews, basil, and mint horizontally along the roll). The easier option is to cut everything up, mix it all together in a bowl, and then you have only one thing to fill the wrappers with (and trust me, it all tastes the same whichever way you decide to go). If you go this easier way, cut the lettuce into bite-sized pieces or julienne strips and mix up with the noodles, cashews, mango, jicama, mint, and basil. Throw in some edible flowers if you'd like.

continues ➡

First, you need to get your wrappers ready to fill. But before you do that, either cut up all the ingredients and have them ready to go, or mix up everything in a bowl. Once the wrappers are dampened, they need to be stuffed and rolled immediately or they can start sticking.

On a baking sheet, add about ½ inch of cool water so you have a place to dip the wrappers as you make them. Working one wrapper at a time, dip the wrapper into the water, making sure the whole thing gets dampened. You don't want to leave the wrapper in the water; it's a dampen-and-go situation. Move the wrapper over to your cutting board, pressing it flat into the board. Start with layering ingredients or placing the mixture in the bottom middle of the wrapper, leaving a 1-inch border at the end closest to you and leaving a 1-inch border on the left and right sides. When the wrapper is just pliable (don't wait too long or it gets too delicate to work with easily), grab the left and right sides of the wrapper and fold over onto the ingredients. Now, take the long side closest to you and lift over the ingredients while carefully tucking them under the wrapper to keep the roll tight. Finish by rolling up the whole thing like a jelly roll.

As you get better at this skill (and you will get better!), play around with adding edible flowers after the first rollover, tucking them horizontally down the roll. By letting them be on their own and toward the last part of the rollup, it's easier to see them through the translucent wrapper. You can also leave some of the ingredients exposed on one end of the roll by tucking them halfway in after the first roll. Leave the rolls whole or cut in half and serve with the black garlic chile sauce.

BLACK GARLIC CHILE SAUCE

This sauce keeps beautifully in the fridge for up to two weeks, so feel free to double the batch.

MAKES ½ CUP

½ cup rice vinegar

½ cup plus 2 tablespoons white sugar

¼ cup water

3 tablespoons gluten-free tamari sauce (or fish sauce)

2 tablespoons sherry wine

3 black garlic cloves or regular, minced

½ to 1 tablespoon crushed red pepper flakes (depending on your heat tolerance)

1½ tablespoons cornstarch dissolved in ¼ cup cool water

Place the rice vinegar, sugar, water, tamari, sherry wine, garlic, and red pepper flakes (all ingredients except the cornstarch-water mixture) into a saucepan or pot and bring to a rolling boil. Reduce the heat to medium and let the sauce gently boil for 10 minutes, or until reduced by half (just over ½ cup). Reduce heat to low and add the cornstarch-water mixture while stirring until the sauce thickens, about 2 minutes. Remove from the heat and have a taste. You should taste sweetness first, followed by sour, then spicy and salty notes. Adjust according to your taste.

kohlrabi

AKA
BRASSICA OLERACEA,
GERMAN TURNIP, TURNIP
CABBAGE, STEM TURNIP

THE 411: If you take the German word *kohl* ("cabbage") and combine it with the word *rübe* or *rabi* ("turnip"), you get "kohlrabi"—or the less sexy name, "cabbageturnip." I'm understanding right now why produce sellers in the United States went with the German name. Kohlrabi resembles a purple or green Trollz doll. At first glance, one wonders how this plant evolved to have stems coming out the side of the vegetable before going up. But we're looking at this vegetable all wrong. Those stems are being pushed out of the way by one extremely overgrown stem, leaving no other choice for the other stems but to go out before going up. Despite the fact that kohlrabi looks a bit like a turnip, kohlrabi is a swollen stem, while turnip is a root. It's this kind of vegetable nerdery that gets me up in the morning.

The first written record of kohlrabi comes from Europe in 1554 by the botanist Mattioli, who let everyone know of this new vegetable that had recently come to Italy. Keep in mind, the first written records do not equate to the first time kohlrabi was discovered or cultivated. Kohlrabi spread to northern Europe and parts of the eastern Mediterranean. Today, kohlrabi is quite popular in eastern India, Hungary, Germany, and northern Vietnam. It is fairly unknown in the US, though it has been more on the radar over the last five years or so, at least in vegetable-happy cities like Seattle, where, if you listen closely, you can hear people asking, "What the hell is *that*?"

Kohlrabi is a member of the cabbage family, and even though turnip is part of its German name, it doesn't have the peppery bite of turnips. It tastes a bit like a broccoli stem or the tender heart of a cabbage, but it's milder and slightly sweeter than either. Young stems can be very juicy and crisp, reminiscent of an apple. The leaves can also be eaten, cooked on their own or along with all the other nutritious greens mentioned in this book: turnip tops, mustard greens, escarole, beet greens, and the like. The rotund stem is typically peeled, and the tender inside can be eaten raw or cooked. In northern Vietnam, kohlrabi (*su hào*) is added to fried spring rolls (*nem rán*) as well as other recipes. In Kashmiri cuisine, where it is called mŏnji, kohlrabi is of central importance. Both stems and leaves are stewed with chiles and served with rice.

AKA: *Brassica oleracea,* German turnip, turnip cabbage, stem turnip.

NUTRITION FACTS: Kohlrabi is full of vitamin C (more than 100 percent of your dietary value in one cup of raw kohlrabi), potassium, folate, and fiber.

SEASON: Kohlrabi does best in cool weather, so while it can be harvested in the fall and spring, winter is when it's at its best.

PURCHASE, STORAGE, AND PREP TIPS: Look for kohlrabi that is about 3 inches in diameter or less, with smooth skin. They should be firm and consistently round; larger ones with elongated stems tend to be woody inside and taste sharper (more radish-like). Smaller ones tend to be more flavorful and sweeter. To store, cut the greens off when you get it home, wrap them with a dry paper towel, and place them in a produce bag. Store the kohlrabi stem loose in the crisper drawer or loosely wrapped in a bag. The greens should be used within a few days, and the stem can be used within a few weeks. Prepping a kohlrabi stem is nearly the same as preparing celery root. Both have a fairly thick skin that is most easily cut off rather than peeled with a vegetable peeler. Cut across the stem end and also on top. Using a chef's knife, slowly make a reverse C cut around the outside. Make sure you are getting off all the peel and cutting into the tender inside. I usually cut the peel off kohlrabi unless it's very young and very tender. The peel is technically edible at any thickness.

COOKING TIPS: Kohlrabi is delightful raw, and you lose some of that great crunch when it's cooked. However, raw vegetables are not for everyone and are harder to digest. To cook kohlrabi stem, keep it al dente to preserve some of its texture and get some nice color on it to highlight its natural sweetness. Young leaves can be eaten raw in salads, but cook older kohlrabi greens until they are tender (they can be a bit more firm than kale or collards, so taste to see if they are tender enough for you before turning the heat off).

SUBS: Stay in the family and sub with cabbage, especially cabbage hearts. Jicama will give you that crunch and sweetness, even if the texture is far less dense. Turnip and radish are more funky and peppery but have a similar texture. A bit out of left field, perhaps, but unripe (green) papaya would make a nice sub; I use kohlrabi in lieu of green papaya (if I can't find green papaya) when making *som tum* (ส้มตำ), a Thai salad, and it is remarkably close in both flavor and texture.

Kohlrabi Slaw *with Apples, Herbs, and Mustard Seed Dressing*

Next time you need a slaw for something, step outside your cabbage coleslaw comfort zone and reach for this easy recipe, which highlights kohlrabi's sweet, crunchy nature and cloaks it in a piquant mustard and apple cider dressing. Serve this slaw on sandwiches; with sausages, meatless or otherwise; atop hot dogs; or alongside fried tomatillos (see Fried Green Tomatillos with Chipotle Comeback Sauce on page 95) or fried okra (see Radha's Okra Bites on page 77).

SERVES 4

FOR THE MUSTARD SEED DRESSING
¼ cup olive oil
2 tablespoons apple cider vinegar
1 tablespoon mayonnaise
1 teaspoon whole grain mustard
¼ teaspoon salt, more if needed
Freshly ground black pepper, to taste

FOR THE SLAW
1 pound kohlrabi
½ teaspoon salt
1 large apple, unpeeled, small diced
½ cup toasted walnuts, roughly chopped
2 tablespoons dill, roughly chopped
2 tablespoons tarragon, roughly chopped

TO MAKE THE DRESSING
Make the vinaigrette by combining all the ingredients in a mason jar and shaking it up just before using it or blending with an immersion blender. Taste the dressing and adjust to your liking.

TO MAKE THE SLAW
Cut the peel off the kohlrabi as directed on page 234. Grate the kohlrabi in a food processor or on the large side of a box grater, or julienne or cut it into thin wedges. If there are young tender greens on the kohlrabi, you can chiffonade (ribbon) them and use them in the slaw. If they are older, use them for cooking.

In a large bowl, add the kohlrabi and salt. Mix well and let it sit for 15 to 30 minutes. Over the sink, squeeze the kohlrabi to remove any excess water. Place the now-squeezed kohlrabi in a medium bowl along with the apple, walnuts, dill, and tarragon. Add the dressing, toss to combine, and season to taste with salt and freshly ground black pepper.

Kohlrabi Salad *with Black Olives, Mint, Orange, and Cotija*

This is a simple weeknight salad that showcases kohlrabi in all of its crunchy, mild, slightly sweet glory. Make twice the dressing if you want to use it on something else during the week. Citrus is in season along with kohlrabi, and they are natural partners. I've offered some subs for you if you can't find cotija cheese. Also feel free to sub out any of the citrus with any other fun citrus that is in season (kumquats, grapefruits, tangerines, and the like).

SERVES 4

FOR THE LEMON VINAIGRETTE
⅓ cup olive oil
¼ cup lemon juice
1 teaspoon honey
½ teaspoon salt
Freshly ground black pepper, to taste

FOR THE SALAD
1 pound kohlrabi
2 navel oranges, peeled, cut into ¼-inch wheels
2 cara cara oranges, peeled, cut into ¼-inch wheels
½ cup mint leaves, roughly chopped or, if small, left whole
½ cup pitted kalamata olives, roughly chopped
½ cup roasted shelled pistachios
2 ounces cotija cheese (or ricotta salata or mizithra cheese)

Make the vinaigrette by combining all the ingredients in a mason jar and shaking it up just before using it or blending with an immersion blender. Taste the vinaigrette and adjust to your liking.

Cut the peel off the kohlrabi as directed on page 234. It's up to you how you want to cut the kohlrabi for this salad. You can grate it on a box grater, put it through the grater blade on your food processor, julienne, or cut it into thin noodle-like ribbons on the mandoline. If there are young tender greens on the kohlrabi, you can chiffonade (ribbon) them and use them in the salad. If they are older, use them for cooking.

In a large bowl, add the kohlrabi, oranges, mint, olives, and pistachios. Pour the dressing on top and mix the salad gently. Taste (get an olive in your taste so you have a more accurate gauge on the salt content) and adjust, as needed. Plate the salad in bowls, garnishing with the cotija cheese.

Glazed Kohlrabi *with Pistachio-Sage Streusel and Parmesan*

I'm serious, my mouth is watering as I'm writing this little note to tell you how this dish will make your mouth water. Nutty brown butter clings to the browned, lightly sweet kohlrabi, cooked until al dente, then topped with a crunchy, slightly cheesy, savory streusel. To really gild the lily, consider frying up the sage leaves to add yet another layer of texture and to bring home the earthy herbal note of the sage in the streusel. This dish is by no stretch hard to make, but because it involves several steps, save it for the weekend when you have a bit more time. If you're not in a kohlrabi mood, try it with turnips, which are also divine served this way.

SERVES 4

FOR THE GLAZED KOHLRABI
1 pound kohlrabi, including leaves (optional)
2 tablespoons unsalted butter
¼ cup shelled pistachios
1 tablespoon olive oil
1 teaspoon salt
¼ cup dry white vermouth or white wine
1 teaspoon honey
2 teaspoons white wine vinegar
¾ cup water
2 cups watercress

FOR THE PISTACHIO-SAGE STREUSEL
Zest of 1 lemon
2 tablespoons minced fresh sage
¼ cup grated Parmesan cheese

FOR THE FRIED SAGE (OPTIONAL)
¼ cup high-heat oil
12 to 16 fried sage leaves (optional)
Flaky salt, as needed

TO MAKE THE KOHLRABI
Cut the peel off the kohlrabi as directed on page 234. Cut the kohlrabi into ¼-inch wedges. Cut any kohlrabi leaves into bite-sized pieces. In a large sauté pan, add the butter and cook over medium heat. Once it melts and starts to foam, add the pistachios. Cook the pistachios in the butter until both start to brown. Scoop the nuts from the butter and reserve, leaving the butter in the pan. Add the kohlrabi and its leaves, if using, to the butter, along with the olive oil and salt. Sear the kohlrabi until it takes on some color and is parcooked (about 5 minutes). Add the vermouth, honey, white wine vinegar, and water and cook for 5 to 7 more minutes, until the kohlrabi is tender and glazed. Mix half of the browned pistachios back into the kohlrabi and keep warm while you make the streusel.

TO MAKE THE STREUSEL

Chop up the remaining pistachios and mix with the lemon zest, sage, and Parmesan cheese.

TO FRY THE SAGE (OPTIONAL)

Heat the oil in a small skillet over medium-high heat until a little piece of sage sizzles (350°F). Fry 6 to 8 sage leaves at a time until crisp, 2 to 3 seconds. Transfer to paper towels and sprinkle with flaky sea salt.

TO ASSEMBLE

Top the kohlrabi with the streusel and optional fried sage leaves. Serve over a bed of watercress.

Rutabaga

AKA
BRASSICA NAPUS VAR.
NAPOBRASSICA, SWEDE,
SWEDISH TURNIP, NEEP,
TURNIP, YELLOW TURNIP

THE 411: Way back when, in 1620—to be precise—a Swiss botanist found a curious plant growing wild in Sweden. That is the first written record of the rutabaga, but it doesn't mean it was the first time it was eaten. Thought to have originated in Russia, Finland, or possibly Scandinavia, it was brought to North America in the early 19th century. Long before pumpkins were used as jack-o'-lanterns, it was the humble rutabaga or possibly a very similar vegetable called a mangel-wurzel (a vegetable just as fun to say as rutabaga). Mangel-wurzel was grown as animal fodder. As far back as the 16th century, youth from the British Isles would hollow out the roots, light them with a burning coal, and go house to house, trading verses for food. If you think Halloween costumes can sometimes be scary, google rutabaga lanterns.

Time for a little review. In the kohlrabi chapter, we learned that even though kohlrabi literally means "cabbageturnip" in German, it's actually a member of the cabbage family and not in the turnip family at all. Rutabaga, on the other hand, is a hybrid between cabbage and turnip, and it's sometimes called turnip, and actually is part turnip. But also part cabbage. In England, they call turnips swedes. In Scotland, rutabagas are called swedes. Is it any wonder why we are confused by these vegetables? Rutabagas look like really big turnips, but where a turnip fades to white from purple, a rutabaga fades to yellow, which is why it's sometimes called yellow turnip. Which leads me to believe that anything that is bulbous and rootlike defaults to turnip. Who is behind BIG TURNIP and how did their lobby get so powerful? The thing is, when I ask Americans what their thoughts are about rutabagas, they literally have no thoughts. Turnips, they have some opinions about. But rutabaga, the most I get is, "I've heard of it . . ." or "It sounds like a food one's great-grandparents would eat."

It seems that rutabaga might possibly be the most ignored and undervalued vegetable in the produce department. Let me ask you a question: If you could have mashed potatoes but have them taste more interesting and have a lot more nutritional value, would you? I'd like to think you would, which is why the traditional Scottish dish "neeps and tatties" (rutabaga and potatoes) is the first recipe in this chapter. Just today I bought a rutabaga at a store outside of Cleveland and also a cool purple sweet potato they were selling. I'm not even kidding—the checker said, "Congratulations, this is by far the ugliest order I've scanned today." Misunderstood vegetable shaming is real.

AKA: *Brassica napus* var. *napobrassica,* swede, Swedish turnip, neep, (confusingly) turnip (Scottish and Canadian English, Irish English, and Manx English), yellow turnip.

Why Do You Need Rutabagas in Your Life?

1. They are inexpensive. Between $1 and $2 a pound!
2. They are extremely nutritious. They are the superfood no one is talking about.
3. They are slightly bittersweet like a good dark chocolate (sweeter than turnips and less sharp) and can be used just like potatoes.
4. They are hardy and keep well (several weeks in your fridge).
5. The Scots call them neeps, which is adorable ("neeps" from the Latin *napus,* which means, naturally, turnip, and here we go again).
6. This list sponsored by BIG RUTABAGA.

NUTRITION FACTS: Rutabagas are off the charts high in vitamin C (one serving contains more than half of your daily dietary needs), plus they are high in fiber, potassium, vitamin B_6, and calcium.

SEASON: A cool-weather vegetable that is planted in the fall and harvested in the winter.

PURCHASE, STORAGE, AND PREP TIPS: Look for firm roots that feel heavy for their size. The thick skin should be smooth, with no soft spots or cuts. Rutabagas will sometimes be coated with wax to prevent them from drying out. I'm not positive, but I think rutabagas are waxed because they don't have a lot of moisture. Rutabagas do keep well. Leave them out at room temperature for up to a week, or for up to two months in places that are around 50°F (a cool basement). If there were greens attached (unusual, unless you got it from a farmers' market or grew it yourself), separate the greens from the root and wrap it in a dry paper towel. Pop the greens into a produce bag.

When you're ready to cook, wash the rutabaga well, dry it, and get ready for some knife work, as you need to cut off the peel. A sharp chef's knife is your friend here for sure. Cut a slice off the bottom and the top. Now that it sits flat on your cutting board, make a reverse C-shaped cut going around the outside of the rutabaga to get all the peel off. You are essentially following the shape of the root as you make your cut, starting at the top, curving the knife as you follow the peel, cutting down the side, and then cutting back inward toward the bottom.

COOKING TIPS: Rutabaga greens can be used as you would mustard, turnip, or radish greens, beet tops, and the like. Rutabaga root takes longer to cook than turnips and potatoes and other root vegetables. To give rutabagas a head start, simply bake or parboil them separately for 10 minutes prior to mixing with other root vegetables.

SUBS: Celery root, turnip, and parsnip all are similarly starchy and can stand in for rutabaga. Daikon radishes, broccoli stems, and kohlrabi can be used, as well.

Neeps and Tatties

This comforting dish has a lot of Scottish history behind it. Neeps and tatties are tradi-tionally served with haggis, a savory, spiced sheep pudding encased in the sheep's stom-ach (there are vegetarian versions). It's a key part of what's known as the Burns supper, a celebratory feast in late January to honor Scotland's national poet, Robert Burns, who famously wrote a poem entitled "Address to a Haggis."

SERVES 4

5 tablespoons plus 1 teaspoon unsalted
   butter
3 tablespoons plus ½ teaspoon salt, divided,
   more as needed
2 pounds russet potatoes, peeled, cut in half
1 pound rutabaga, peeled, small cubed
1 tablespoon high-heat oil
Freshly ground black pepper, to taste

Preheat the oven to 450°F. Line a baking sheet with parchment paper, making sure the paper doesn't go over the edge. Rub a 9-by-11-inch casserole dish with 1 teaspoon of the butter.

Fill a pot with water to boil the potatoes. Add 3 tablespoons of salt to the water. Add the potatoes and bring to a boil. Turn down the heat to maintain a simmer and cook the potatoes until a knife slips easily in and out, about 15 minutes. Drain the potatoes through a colander.

Place the rutabaga on the baking sheet. Toss with the oil, spread the rutabaga back out, and sprinkle the ½ teaspoon salt over the top. Pop in the oven and roast until browned and tender, about 20 minutes. Put the potatoes through a ricer, if you have one; if not, mash them well with a potato masher. Use a masher to smash the ruta-baga cubes (they don't go easily through a ricer because of their dry consistency). Add both to a bowl together, add 3 tablespoons of the butter, mix, add more salt to taste, and then place in the casserole dish and dot with the remaining 2 tablespoons butter on top. Crack some black pepper on top. Pop in the oven to reheat and melt the butter, about 5 minutes. Serve right away.

Rutabaga Remoulade

Traditionally a remoulade is a mayonnaise-based French sauce, typically folded into a salad made with only celery root. The addition here of rutabaga makes a more complex and definitely more nutritious version of the classic. It would be lovely served over Radicchio Insalata Mista (page 45), garnished with toasted walnuts. Or you could serve this in an avocado half as a light lunch.

SERVES 4

1½ teaspoons salt

1 pound rutabaga, peeled, grated in a food processor (or on the large side of a box grater)

½ pound celery root, peeled, grated in a food processor (or on the large side of a box grater)

½ Granny Smith apple, cut into short matchsticks

6 tablespoons mayonnaise

1 tablespoon lemon juice, plus more to taste

1 tablespoon Dijon mustard

1 tablespoon capers, chopped

1 tablespoon tarragon leaves, roughly chopped

2 tablespoons parsley leaves, roughly chopped

¼ cup toasted walnuts, chopped (optional)

Salt the grated rutabaga and celery root and let sit for 15 minutes, then squeeze out all the liquid. In a medium bowl, combine the rutabaga and celery root with the apple. In another bowl, whisk together the mayonnaise, lemon juice, mustard, capers, tarragon, and parsley. Fold the dressing into the vegetables. Taste and adjust according to your liking. Garnish with the toasted walnuts.

Rutabaga Gnocchi *with Crispy Sage, Hazelnuts, and Roasted Apples*

Gnocchi can be intimidating to make when the skill is new to you. But once mastered, it's incredibly fun to form the pieces, satisfying to cut and brown them, and especially gratifying to eat. The best gnocchi uses just enough flour to hold them together, super dry potatoes (baked), and a gentle technique that develops the gluten just enough to keep the gnocchi pillowy. In this recipe, we're subbing rutabaga for some of the potatoes to add complexity of flavor and a boost to the nutritional profile. This recipe can easily be doubled and frozen for a dinner on another day.

SERVES 4

FOR THE GNOCCHI

1 pound russet potatoes (about 2 medium)
1 pound rutabaga, peeled, large diced
2 tablespoons olive oil, divided
1 egg, beaten
¾ cup all-purpose flour, plus additional as needed
2 tablespoons plus 1 teaspoon salt, divided, more if needed
2 tablespoons high-heat oil

FOR THE GARNISHES AND SAUCE

⅓ cup hazelnuts, for garnish
2 tart-sweet apples (such as Honeycrisp or Pink Lady), unpeeled, medium diced
½ red onion, cut into thin half-moons
4 tablespoons unsalted butter
20 sage leaves
1½ teaspoons white wine vinegar
Freshly ground black pepper, to taste

TO MAKE THE GNOCCHI AND BAKE THE NUTS AND APPLES

Preheat the oven to 350°F.

Pierce the potatoes all over with the tines of a fork. Bake them in the oven directly on a rack for about 1½ hours, flipping them after 45 minutes, until they are tender, dry, and have crackly skins. Meanwhile, lay the rutabaga on a parchment-lined baking sheet and toss with 1 tablespoon of the olive oil. Pop into the oven with the potatoes and cook the rutabaga until it's tender, about 30 minutes. Take advantage of the hot oven to get some other prep done: On a baking sheet, toast the hazelnuts in the oven until lightly browned, about 10 to 12 minutes. Rub the hazelnuts in a towel to remove some of the dark brown skin. Set the hazelnuts aside. Using the same baking sheet that the hazelnuts were on, pop those apples and red onion onto the tray, toss with the other tablespoon of olive oil, and roast until lightly browned and tender,

continues ➡

25 to 30 minutes. Set the apples and onions aside. Give those hazelnuts a quick rough chop or tap them with the bottom of a glass (my preferred technique) and set aside.

FINISHING THE GNOCCHI PREP

When the potatoes are ready and still hot (and using towels to protect yourself), cut them in half and use a spoon to scoop out the centers. Discard the potato skins or eat with sour cream (mmmm). Run the potato through a ricer or food mill, and mash the rutabaga really well by hand. Combine them and spread out on a baking sheet to cool.

When the potato-rutabaga mixture is cool, transfer to a large bowl and stir in the egg, flour, and 1 teaspoon salt. Mix well with a wooden spoon and then knead the dough gently in the bowl until it forms a ball, adding more flour if necessary (but keep in mind the more flour you add, the tougher the gnocchi will be). Transfer the dough to a wooden board and divide it into 8 pieces. Roll each piece into a long rope about ¾ inch in diameter.

When all the pieces are rolled out, cut each rope into gnocchi approximately ¾ inch long. Toss these pieces through some flour and then shake off the excess and place them on a parchment-lined baking sheet.

To freeze the gnocchi for later use, place them on a parchment-lined baking sheet (make sure they are not touching each other) and put them in the freezer for about 1 hour. When the gnocchi are frozen, transfer them to a freezer bag and use within 3 months.

To cook the gnocchi, bring a large pot of water to a boil. Add the 2 tablespoons of salt and cook the gnocchi (in two batches), removing them after they have floated to the surface plus about 1 minute.

FINISHING THE DISH

Heat a large skillet over medium-high heat. Add the butter and, when it's almost melted, add the sage leaves and cook them in the butter until the butter browns and the sage leaves have darkened a bit in color and crisped up, about 4 to 5 minutes. Scoop out the sage leaves and place them on a piece of paper towel and set aside for garnish. Add the gnocchi to the pan and fry in the butter until browned, about 3 to 4 minutes. When all the gnocchi are browned, add the apples and onions and hazelnuts to the pan. Toss it all together, coating everything with the butter. Add the vinegar and black pepper, mix, and taste for seasoning, adding salt as needed. Serve the gnocchi, garnishing each bowl with some fried sage leaves.

Turnip

AKA
BRASSICA RAPA SUBSP. RAPA,
TOKYO TURNIP, JAPANESE
TURNIP, HAKUREI TURNIP

THE 411: Turnips are just a stone's throw, relatively speaking, from radishes, rapini, and Brussels sprouts, among others. They are all in the *Brassica* genus, and if I were to synthesize in a few words what these vegetables bring to the world, I'd have to say they show up with the funk and the spice. They are more than just that, of course. Turnips are typically cooked more than eaten raw, but even when heat is applied, gently coaxing out its sweetness, there is still that powerful bass note, that zesty, hits-you-in-the-nose bite. Brassicas take no guff from no one. It is in appreciating this aspect of turnips, and knowing how to balance it, where the magic is made and where all the misunderstandings are cleared up.

Turnips are as old as the hills, and wild forms have been found all over western Asia and Europe. First cultivated—perhaps—in northern Europe (Siberia), turnips eventually made their way to China and Japan around A.D. 700. In more modern times, turnips were a significant food crop of antebellum America, both for the root and the greens. Turnip greens were cooked with salt pork, and the ensuing broth was (and is) called potlikker. Coarse cornmeal was cooked into cakes (corn pone) and crumbled or dunked into the broth. (There is much debate about whether it was crumbled or dunked, not to mention the correct spelling of *potlikker*). Suffice it to say, the history of turnips in America has a lot to do with an easy-to-grow crop that provided both a root and greens that held up through the winter and could sustain an awful lot of Americans (Indigenous Americans, southerners generally, and Black southerners specifically) when not much else was growing.

There are over 30 varieties of turnips, but the ones we are most likely to see in the markets are the purple-topped ones as well as the smaller "baby" turnips. Baby turnips come in many colors, from white to orange, yellow, and even red-fleshed. The smaller turnips tend to be milder than their larger sisters and are the preferred choice for eating raw.

AKA: *Brassica rapa* subsp. *rapa*, Tokyo turnip, Japanese turnip, Hakurei turnip.

NUTRITION FACTS: High in vitamin C, other antioxidants, and copper.

SEASON: Turnips are available all year, but winter or late fall is the best time to enjoy them. You can even enjoy them in the spring, when they are sweet and small.

PURCHASE, STORAGE, AND PREP TIPS: Look for small turnips (which in the case of the familiar purple-topped varieties will be younger) or "baby" turnips, which are varieties that come in many colors. These will be the most tender with the best texture and the most sweetness. Older, larger turnips get woodier and spicier and have thicker skins. Make sure they are firm, with no cuts or soft spots. If there are greens attached, they should be fresh looking, nice and bright, and not be wilted or shriveled at all. Turnips will keep in the fridge well wrapped in produce bags for up to two weeks. Larger turnips require some peeling, but tender, smaller ones (and any of the so-called baby varieties) do not need to be peeled. Make sure to clean turnips (and especially the greens) very well, cut off any dangling roots, and proceed to cut to the size you need for the recipe.

COOKING TIPS: The zippiness and pepper of turnips mellows when cooking and those natural sugars get concentrated. Cook until the turnips are easily pierced with a knife. Turnip greens can be cooked as you would kale, collards, or mustard greens. In fact, saving turnip greens and using them in any of the mustard greens recipes in this book would work quite well. Cook those greens! I don't think I need to tell you how good they are for you, but you might be surprised at how delicious they are. Simply wash well and sauté in butter or oil. Add broth if you want, salt to taste, and a splash of vinegar.

SUBS: Daikon radish is a really nice substitute for turnips. It's got the funk. It brings the peppery heat. Ditto for radish. Other possibilities: parsnip, rutabaga, kohlrabi, or parsley root.

Caramelized Turnip Stuffing *with Cranberries, Apples, Turnip Greens, and White Beans*

I'm going to give you permission to make just this one thing tonight. It's not a side dish, it's the dish. Life can be hard. Open up a bottle of red wine, slap that cast-iron skillet down on the table, and pull up a chair. Or embrace the darkness of winter, let the TV be your light, and eat this on the couch right from the pan. Don't burn your lap. While officially the stars of this dish are the buttery, tender turnips—and as the costar their slightly peppery greens, provided you were able to score some attached to the root—the unofficial stars are the bread bits. The bread absorbs much of the delectable drippings from the glorious bounty, getting crusty in some parts, tender in other parts. It's the perfect soul-soothing carb comfort, just right for those dark days when it's just you and a whole pan of food.

SERVES 4

¼ cup olive oil
1½ pounds baby turnips with greens
   (if possible)
4 ounces crusty bread, medium diced
1 large carrot, cut into 1-inch pieces
4 ounces shallot, cut into thick ½-inch rings
One 15-ounce can white beans, drained
1 Fuji (or other tart-sweet) apple, unpeeled,
   large diced
1 cup fresh or frozen cranberries
¼ cup hard apple cider or dry white wine
1 teaspoon salt
Pinch crushed red pepper flakes
4 tablespoons unsalted butter
1 orange, zested and juiced
¼ cup parsley, roughly chopped
2 tablespoons toasted pine nuts

Preheat the oven to 400°F.

Add the olive oil to a large cast-iron skillet (or other oven-safe skillet). Cut off the turnip tops. Wash the greens and cut into ribbons. Set aside. Peel the turnips and cut into halves if they are quite small or quarters if they are bigger. Scatter the bread on top of the oil in the pan. Top the bread with the turnips, carrots, shallots, beans, apples, and cranberries. Drizzle the cider on top. Sprinkle everything with salt and crushed red pepper flakes. Dot the dish with the butter. Cover with foil and bake for 45 minutes. Uncover the foil, add the orange zest and juice and turnip greens if you have them, give everything a mix, and continue to cook until the turnips are tender and caramelized, 10 to 15 minutes more. Garnish with the parsley and pine nuts.

Rice Cake Soup *with Turnips, Mushrooms, and Spicy Chile Oil*

This recipe is based on tteokguk, *a dish eaten in Korea to bring in the Lunar New Year. Traditionally garnished with meat, this version replaces the meat with earthy mushrooms and sweet, slightly funky (in the best way) roasted turnips. If you're unfamiliar with sliced rice cakes, they can be found in most Asian markets in the frozen foods section. Think of them as deliciously chewy gluten-free dumplings. They add a wonderful texture to the soup and (bonus) are super easy to work with: simply thaw, soak, and then cook for just a few minutes.*

SERVES 4

1 pound turnips (baby turnips if available), plus greens, sliced, if they look good

1 tablespoon high-heat oil, plus 1 teaspoon for cooking eggs

¼ teaspoon salt, plus more to taste

1 ounce dried mushrooms (shiitake and porcini are especially good for this)

2 cups boiling water plus 2 quarts cool water, divided

4 grams (0.2 ounces) kombu

2 tablespoons gluten-free tamari (or soy sauce)

4 green onions, white and light green parts cut into 1-inch lengths, greens thinly cut on the bias, for garnish

1 pound frozen Korean sliced rice cakes, thawed and soaked in cold water for 20 minutes

3 eggs, yolks and whites separated

1 teaspoon sesame oil, divided

8 ounces dried rice vermicelli noodles, prepared as directed on page 228)

About ¼ cup Spicy Chile Oil (page 188)

Preheat the oven to 425°F. Line a baking sheet with parchment paper.

Peel the turnips and cut into bite-sized wedges. Toss the turnips with 1 tablespoon of the oil and then season with salt. Place on the baking sheet and roast until tender and lightly browned, about 20 minutes.

Meanwhile, place the mushrooms in a French press if you have one or in a tall container. Pour about 2 cups of boiling water over the top (and depress the plunger if you are using a French press). Let the mushrooms rehydrate. When soft, pull the mushrooms out of the liquid and then carefully strain the liquid so no grit gets through, saving the strained liquid. Cut the mushrooms into bite-sized slices and place in a soup pot along with the strained mushroom soaking liquid, kombu, and 2 quarts of water. Gently bring the heat up until it's at the gentlest simmer, about 5 minutes. Remove the kombu, slice into thin julienne strips, and set aside for garnish.

Add the tamari to the pot along with the

white part of the green onions and cook for another 10 minutes. When the turnips are done, add them to the soup along with any sliced turnip greens. Cook for another 10 minutes and taste for seasoning. Add salt to taste. Add the rice cakes and bring back to the boil. Turn down the heat and simmer for 2 to 3 minutes, just until the rice cakes bob to the surface and have lost their starchiness. Taste again and adjust to your liking.

Meanwhile, in two small bowls, whisk up the yolks and whites separately and add ½ teaspoon sesame oil to each bowl plus a pinch of salt. Heat up a small nonstick skillet over medium-high heat. Add 1 teaspoon of the high-heat oil to the pan and pour out the whites into the pan, turning the pan to coat the surface with the egg whites. When it has firmed up on the bottom but not browned, carefully flip the egg white "crêpe" over and cook the other side for just a moment longer. Slide out onto a cutting board and, when cool, roll it up and slice into thin strips. Repeat this same process with the egg yolks.

Serve the soup to each person with small bowls of egg white, egg yolk, kombu, vermicelli, spicy chile oil, and green onion for garnish.

Smoky Baby Turnips
with Pistachio-Herb Vinaigrette

My friend Seddy (Sedrick Livingston) is a badass chef who is as sweet as a teddy bear, and he wouldn't shy away from that description either. We both grew up in Jersey (albeit 30 years apart), and when he returned to Seattle from a trip home, he brought me some pork roll (Taylor ham) because he knows what's good. Delancey, the famed pizza place where he's been the managing chef for the past few years, shares walk-in space with The Pantry, the cooking school I teach at from time to time. One day I opened the walk-in and the smell of sweetness, funk, woodsmoke, and char hit me full on in the face. I turned around, walked back out, tracked Seddy down. "What is that gloriousness you have in there?" And this man, who loves his pork roll, had built a vegetarian dish around the most funkily fantastic woodsmoked baby turnips. It was a revelation, and it is with his permission that I took that idea and put my own twist on it.

SERVES 4

1 pound baby turnips
2 tablespoons unsalted butter
1 teaspoon salt, divided, plus more to taste
1 cup arugula
½ cup pistachios, toasted
1 tablespoon marjoram leaves
2 tablespoons white wine vinegar
1 tablespoon honey
½ cup olive oil
1 tablespoon black sesame seeds
¼ teaspoon flaky salt

Preheat the oven to 450°F.

*TO MAKE THIS DISH IN A SMOKER
OR GRILL AND FINISH IN THE OVEN:*

I recommend using applewood pellets, chips, or wood for this dish. Trim and peel the turnips. Cook the turnips whole in your smoker or on your grill with smoking wood until the turnips are infused with wood-smoke flavor, depending on the size, about 15 to 25 minutes. Slice off a thin piece and taste one to see if it is nice and smoky. Then cut them in half or in quarters, depending on the size. Melt the butter in a cast-iron skillet or oven-safe skillet over medium heat. Add the turnips, cut side down, and sprinkle with ½ teaspoon of the salt. Pop in the oven and cook until they are tender and golden brown

continues ➡

in places, 10 to 15 minutes (depending on the size of the turnip pieces).

TO MAKE THIS DISH ENTIRELY
IN THE OVEN:
Trim and peel the turnips. You will be pre-cooking the turnips in the oven and applying smoke after the fact. Roast the trimmed turnips whole on a baking sheet until they are crisp tender, about 15 to 25 minutes, depending on the size. Use a smoking gun (follow manufacturer's instructions) or Japanese smoke wood (that you can order online). To use Japanese smoke wood, you'll need a roasting pan with a cooling rack in it. Break or cut off a small piece of the log. Light it and place it on some foil in the bottom of the pan. Put the turnips on the cooling rack and cover the pan with foil but not tightly so that the smoke wood keeps producing smoke. You can do this outside. Let the smoke fill the pan and scent the turnips. Taste one after about 15 minutes.

Make sure it tastes nice and smoky. Cut the turnips in half or quarters depending on the size. Melt the butter in a cast-iron skillet or oven-safe skillet over medium heat. Add the turnips, cut side down, and sprinkle with ½ teaspoon of the salt. Pop back in the oven and cook until they are tender and golden brown in places, 10 to 15 minutes (depending on the size of the turnip pieces).

While the turnips are cooking, make the vinaigrette by blending ¾ cup of the arugula along with half of the pistachios, the remaining ½ teaspoon salt, marjoram, vinegar, honey, and olive oil. Blend well. Season to taste with salt. Grind the sesame seeds with the remaining pistachios in a mortar and pestle or spice grinder until broken up but still with a little texture. Mix in the flaky salt. Spoon the vinaigrette on the platter. Lay the turnips on the vinaigrette. Garnish with the pistachio-sesame-salt mixture and the remaining arugula leaves.

More Misunderstood Vegetables Quiz

How many of these 30 other misunderstood vegetables have you tried?
Check the boxes below:

☐ Black garlic	☐ Chayote	☐ Lotus root
☐ Ramps	☐ Salsify	☐ Fiddlehead ferns
☐ Cactus paddles	☐ Cardoon	☐ Parsley root
☐ Crosnes	☐ White asparagus	☐ Horseradish
☐ Dandelion greens	☐ Yucca	☐ Oca
☐ Sea beans	☐ Dulse	☐ Broccoli rabe
☐ Water spinach	☐ Bitter melon	☐ Scorzonera
☐ Chinese long beans	☐ Tatsoi	☐ Chrysanthemum
☐ Taro	☐ Winter melon	☐ Gai lan
☐ Garlic scapes	☐ Bamboo shoots	☐ Hearts of palm

IF YOU'VE TRIED 10 OR LESS: You have an adventurous palate!

IF YOU'VE TRIED 11 TO 29: You have an extremely adventurous palate, and my guess is that you've been lucky enough to travel a lot.

IF YOU'VE TRIED ALL 30: Congratulations, you get to write *More Misunderstood Vegetables*!

Acknowledgments

Thank you to Clare Barboza, my ride-or-die photographer, without whom I cannot even conceive of writing a cookbook, and to Joe Barboza and Hugo for being my family away from home at Clare's Vermont studio. Abby Canfield (Lady Lord Abigail Confield of the Hanover Confields), my friend and co-chef on the M/V *Thea Foss,* has been a huge source of support, advice, and hands-on help throughout this project, and I am endlessly grateful for her ear, creativity, and her most beautiful beet salad. Ashlyn Forshner's place on Whidbey Island is my writing retreat and home away from home, and our culinary collaborations make my books something I'm proud of. Thank you to Matthew Amster-Burton for his sage suggestions to the introduction and for introducing me to the wonders of charred cabbage. Special thanks to Sara Armstrong and Monica Verastegui: this book wouldn't be here had they not suggested I write it. Heather Weiner and Carma Clark, aka Test Kitchen Central, Bella Ciao Pandemic Family, Below Deck–hands, thank you for your always willing palates, great feedback, and the best test garden produce ever.

Thank you to Brandi Henderson, The Pantry Cooking School, my colleagues and my students who attended my Misunderstood Vegetables classes, Kerri Bates for being so supportive of my need for writing time, Rose Laughlin for supporting her local author, Gretchen Rude for photo shoot shopping, and Miranda Hall for going the extra mile (literally) and gathering squash blossoms at Harlow Farms for the photo shoot.

Endless thanks to my family: Jeremy Selengut for his thoroughness in being a careful reader of many of the science-leaning portions of this book and his careful and joyful attention in testing many of the recipes, and Jesse Selengut and Deborah Hardt for testing many of the vegan recipes in their adopted hometown of Izmir, Turkey. Radha Friedman, your deft hand with vegetables and gluten-free and vegan cooking is inspiring, and I knew you'd make an excellent tester. Thank you for your friendship and culinary generosity. Thank you to Dr. Jessica Harris for taking the time to read my okra chapter and offer some sage quotes.

To my tasting team, thank you for your feedback: Alex Selengut, Micah Selengut, Jessica Sunshine, Helen Salz, Jeffrey Sunshine, Dasha Keig, Ari Sunshine, Melissa Hou, Kerrin Sunshine, Kathleen Eder, Sarah Dijulio, and Steve Hawkins.

Thanks to my agent, Sharon Bowers,

for having my back, taking my calls and questions, and being a source of wisdom and advice throughout.

Thank you to Ann Treistman, my editor at Countryman Press, for her deft hand with the edits, truly the key to producing a cookbook worth its weight on one's bookshelf. Thank you also to the following people at Countryman for their hard work and dedication: Zachary Polendo, publicity; Devorah Backman, marketing; Devon Zahn, production; Jess Murphy, managing editorial; Allison Chi, design; and Maya Goldfarb, editorial assistant. Thank you to Diane Durrett for her copyediting prowess and eagle-eyed attention to the details that are everything when it comes to making a recipe make sense to the reader.

To my beautiful wife, April, for being so supportive and understanding of all the hours and time away one needs to write a book. You're my number one.

Index

Gluten-Free Recipes

Vegan Recipes

General Index

About the Author

BECKY SELENGUT is an educator and chef based in Seattle. She is the chef on the M/V *Thea Foss* and the author of four other books: *Good Fish, Shroom, How to Taste,* and *Not One Shrine*. Selengut forages, makes a mean Manhattan, and shares her life with her sommelier wife, April Pogue, and their lovably loony pointer mix, Izzy. [© MARK HENESY]

About the Photographer

CLARE BARBOZA is a New England–based food photographer who works with food brands and publishers from all over the country. Her background is in fine art and her passion lies in telling stories, particularly stories about how food goes from the farm to the kitchen to the table. Clare is also the co-owner of Poppy Bee Surfaces, which she runs with her husband, making beautiful, lightweight photo backgrounds for food and product shoots. [© CLARE BARBOZA]